*methodism's
destiny
in an
ecumenical age*

methodism's destiny in an ecumenical age

paul m. minus, jr., editor

ABINGDON PRESS
NASHVILLE
NEW YORK

SET UP, PRINTED, AND BOUND BY THE
PARTHENON PRESS, AT NASHVILLE,
TENNESSEE, UNITED STATES OF AMERICA

foreword

John Wesley once remarked that he welcomed the participation of predestinarians in his societies as long as they were not contentious about their opinions. As one with such a predestinarian pedigree I appreciate traditional Methodist openness, and will exercise care to abide by Wesley's ground rules!

One of the opportunities of the ecumenical movement (and one of its prerequisites if it is to fulfill its unique potential) is frank and free discussion by Christians of each tradition about past positions, present frustrations, and future possibilities. Necessary in any such discussion is broadly based concern and participation, with insights received from and communicated to as large a part of the constituency as possible.

The essays which follow represent exactly such necessary denominational pulse-taking and prescription. Here are found the elements of the necessary discussion: an appreciation of past Methodist ecumenical initiative and contributions combined with a calling into question of present or future foot-dragging; an awareness and appreciation of Methodism as a world family, but a corresponding realization of the attendant dangers of confessional imperialism with its resulting frustration of deeper local ecumenicity; a theological assessment of its genuine ecumenical treasure; a sensitivity to the fact that all mission in today's world requires an understanding of and identification with the "revolutions" of men—that mission looks to humanization; and finally, a concern that in the midst of fresh theological trends and insights, the traditional Methodist zeal for communicating the person and significance of Jesus Christ may be continued as the foundation and ultimate goal of the entire undertaking.

The next decade represents a critical time for the worldwide movement of ecumenical renewal. Churches of all traditions are understanding and experiencing the concepts of catholicity, apostolicity, and unity in new ways. As Roman Catholic participation becomes continually more possible and necessary, how shall a conciliar structure be fashioned which embodies the gift of catholicity in both its local and worldwide dimensions? Evidences of genuine Christian community are now being recognized in activities and patterns formerly thought to be unrelated to the existence of the church; ethical positions, such as hatred of racism and involvement in development, are also elements of apostolicity. We are realizing, too, that some ecclesiastical structures once thought to exhibit the supranational unity of the church have actually served, by their insensitive paternalism and ecclesiastical colonialism, to destroy that unity.

The *full* significance and consequence of such concepts is not to be grasped by attempting to reproduce some form once existing in history, but rather is even now being discovered and brought to new depth and reality through our common work together. This is simply to say that not only is the destiny of Methodism to be seen ecumenically (as is so well stated in these pages), but also that the destiny of the churches, if they are to fulfill their mission in and to the οἰκουμένη, is truly an ecumenical one.

EUGENE CARSON BLAKE

the contributors

Eugene Carson Blake: *General Secretary, World Council of Churches.*

Rupert E. Davies: *Principal, Wesley College, Bristol, England.*

Francis Gerald Ensley: *Resident Bishop, the Ohio West Area of The United Methodist Church; President, the American Section of the World Methodist Council.*

Theressa Hoover: *Associate General Secretary, Board of Missions, The United Methodist Church.*

José Miguez-Bonino: *President, Union Theological Seminary, Buenos Aires, Argentina.*

Paul S. Minear: *Winkley Professor of Biblical Theology, Yale University.*

Paul M. Minus, Jr.: *Associate Professor of Church History, Methodist Theological School in Ohio.*

Walter G. Muelder: *Dean and Professor of Social Ethics, Boston University School of Theology.*

D. T. Niles: *Chairman, East Asia Christian Conference; President, the Methodist Church of Ceylon.*

Albert C. Outler: *Professor of Theology, Perkins School of Theology, Southern Methodist University.*

Alan Walker: *Superintendent, Central Methodist Mission, Sydney, Australia.*

To the memory of
John R. Mott
(1865-1955)

contents

introduction

The Methodist movement burst upon eighteenth-century England as a promising bearer of fresh spiritual life. Today, after more than two centuries of activity, it is found in eighty-six countries around the world. The forty-three million Methodists in those lands increasingly feel the impact of another, younger movement: the ecumenical movement sparks hope among Christians everywhere that their ranks can be closed and the church made a prophetic and healing force in a torn world. Methodists, like Christians in other denominational families, now must determine their stance toward the ecumenical movement. How shall the heirs of the earlier renewal respond to the challenges posed by the newer one? To help Methodists grapple with that question is the chief purpose of this book.

They might well begin by acknowledging that the churches have entered an ecumenical era. Growing numbers of Christians throughout the world know that they share a common inheritance, a common task, and a common destiny. That conviction *moves* the ecumenical movement. It stirs clergy and laity alike to seek to make the gospel of reconciliation fully effectual within the Christian community, thereby overcoming the mutual isolation and estrangement that long have marked it. That conviction moreover emboldens them to announce to the world that the reconciliation occurring in their midst is fundamentally God's doing and that he invites the whole human family to its joys and responsibilities.

The signs of this common Christian endeavor are manifold and widespread. Since 1925, 149 denominations have merged to form united churches (e.g. in 1965 the United Church of Zambia was formed by a merger of the Church of Central Africa in Rhodesia, the Church of Barotseland, Free Churches in the Copperbelt, and the Methodist Church). Another 118 denominations currently are considering such union.[1] Innumerable councils of churches—local, state, national, regional, and global—sponsor dialogue and cooperative action among Christians across denominational boundaries. The Roman Catholic Church, the largest of the Christian bodies, has become an active (albeit belated) participant in many ecumenical ventures. Denominations regularly seek the fellowship and counsel of each other. Persons from widely divergent traditions join in common worship. And less evident (but no less important), Christians correct their caricatures of each other, replace mutual prejudice with mutual respect, and relearn the most fundamental lesson of all: "Love one another."

Successful as the ecumenical movement has been, its past victories must not be overstated or its present strength overestimated. Some denominations have chosen not to participate in ecumenical activities. Resistance to all forms of ecumenism remains strong among a vocal minority. Large numbers of persons in denominations officially related to ecumenical organizations are uninformed and indifferent. Some church leaders have difficulty breaking with accus-

[1] M. D. Handspicker, "Church Union Negotiations," in *World Christian Handbook 1968*, H. W. Coxill and Kenneth Grubb, eds. (Nashville: Abingdon Press, 1967), pp. 33-47; the *Handbook's* information is updated in "Survey of Church Union Negotiations, 1965-1967," *The Ecumenical Review*, XX (July, 1968), 263-92, and in two unpublished World Council of Churches documents: "Church Unions Consummated Since 1925" and "Negotiations For Organic Union Now Under Way" (May, 1968).

tomed and tested denominational procedures in favor of unfamiliar and risky ecumenical ones. Honest theological differences persist across traditional denominational boundaries. New rifts have emerged within the churches, many of them reflecting fresh or deepened divisions in society. Moreover, among persons firmly committed to the ecumenical movement, disagreement is evident regarding the movement's ultimate goal and appropriate next steps.

Nevertheless, after all these facts have been noted, it seems likely that the dominant pressures operating upon and within the churches will continue to move them toward greater unity. What forms their unity should take, however, remains an open and urgent question.

Methodists have been regular travelers in the ecumenical voyage. At some times and in some places their participation has been notable. Methodists of different denominations in the same country have united their forces, as in the British "union" of 1932 and the American "unification" of 1939. Some have created united churches with non-Methodist denominations, such as the United Church of Canada (1925) and the already mentioned United Church of Zambia (1965). Presently nineteen Methodist denominations around the world are involved in negotiations leading to possible union. Councils of churches typically enjoy the support and participation of Methodists.

The most striking sign of Methodist ecumenical involvement is the distinguished leadership given ecumenical ventures by Methodists. One such leader outranks all others —John Raleigh Mott (1865-1955). Layman, world evangelist, ecclesiastical statesman, Nobel Peace Prize winner, "the pioneer of the modern ecumenical movement" [2]—Mott towers as one of the great Christians of the twentieth century. The international ecumenical organizations whose founding and growth he decisively influenced (the World's Student Christian Federation, the International Missionary Council, the World Alliance of the Young Men's Christian Association, and the World Council of Churches) are only the most obvious realm of his wide impact. With gratitude for his vision and his accomplishment, this volume is dedicated to the memory of Dr. Mott.

It must be admitted, however, that the record of Methodism's ecumenical involvement is checkered and its present mood ambivalent. The latter fact is attested by one American Methodist official's honest admission: "In one meeting we vote a million dollars to support an ecumenical project, and the next week we wish we had it back." [3] The signs and causes of Methodist uncertainty are suggested in the following essays. Reading them may tempt some Methodists to compare the Methodist ecumenical ledger with those of other confessional families. Such "comparative ecumenics" easily leads one to conclude either that "we do better than they do," or that "we do no worse than they do." Whether or not such conclusions are accurate, they give scant help in answering the question now crucial for Methodists: What does God intend for *Methodism* in an ecumenical age?

The authors of the following essays are eminently qualified to deal with the multiple facets of that question. All have

[2] These are the words of Ruth Rouse, in A *History of the Ecumenical Movement, 1517-1948*, Ruth Rouse and Stephen Neill, eds. (Philadelphia: Westminster Press, 1954), p. 331.

[3] Tracey K. Jones, Jr., quoted in *Together*, November, 1966, p. 14.

been keenly involved in the ecumenical movement, and its impact upon them (especially that of the 1968 Uppsala Assembly of the World Council of Churches) is apparent. They also hold highly responsible positions in their own denominations. All but one are Methodists.

Professor Minear's opening essay is a candid, penetrating statement of the challenge posed by ecumenism to all Christians—but especially to Methodists. The subsequent essays reflect both agreement and disagreement with his positions. Professor Outler's chapter places the roots of a key Methodist doctrinal emphasis deep within the Christian tradition and points to its contemporary import for Wesley's theological heirs. Bishop Ensley and President Miguez-Bonino, approaching the question of world Methodism from service in different areas of the world, reveal significantly different perspectives. Principal Davies, Dr. Niles, Dean Muelder, and Miss Hoover discuss current ecumenical issues facing Methodists in their respective lands and thereby share insight and experience applicable well beyond those lands. The symposium is ended by Dr. Walker's strong stress upon the missionary note that runs through all the essays.

Many issues arise in these pages. Four especially important ones recur frequently. Individual authors suggest their answers, and among some there is a significant convergence of thought. But no unanimously accepted answers emerge. These issues now deserve high priority on the agenda of Methodist thought and debate.[4]

[4] That comparable issues are important among other churches now facing their ecumenical responsibility is suggested in "Survey of Church Union Negotiations," pp. 263-64.

1. Does the main line of Methodist ecumenical advance lead toward the creation of organically united churches with other denominations in the same nation? If so, what shape should such churches take? Is this the way of faithfulness to the church's Lord or of submission to the alluring powers of our time?

2. Is there a distinctive Methodist contribution, born of our particular history, that should be preserved for and offered to the church universal? If so, what is that contribution? How is it appropriately maintained, nurtured, and communicated in an ecumenical age?

3. Should Methodist denominations around the world be linked in an international Methodist body? If so, what exactly will be its purpose, structure, and authority? Would membership in such a body and participation in an organically united church be complementary or alternative courses for a particular denomination?

4. How can the concerns and structures of the traditional ecumenical movement ("ecclesiastical ecumenism") be most creatively related to the vision and style of those persons from many churches who, in the name of Christ, venture together into the world beyond established denominational and interdenominational landmarks ("secular ecumenism")? How does God's redemptive activity in and through the churches relate to his redemptive work outside them?

The urgency of these questions can scarcely be overstressed. Historic decisions soon must be made by Methodist bodies considering organic union. In 1969, for example, the British Methodist Church will decide if it wishes to unite with the Church of England. During the 1970's The United Methodist Church (itself the result of a recent merger between The Methodist and the Evangelical United Brethren Churches) will help design the American-based united church now envisaged in the Consultation on Church Union; by the end of that decade United Methodists likely will have determined whether they are to be a part of the new church. The three predominantly Negro American Methodist bodies—also involved in the Consultation—face a similar prospect. The traditional patterns of Methodism could be radically altered by such unions; indeed, Methodism as a distinct organized entity could eventually disappear. Decision on such weighty matters will be made responsibly to the degree that Methodists approach them in the light of the best thinking available about the gospel, Methodism, ecumenism, and today's world.

These essays were first presented at a symposium in September, 1968, celebrating the tenth anniversary of the founding of the Methodist Theological School in Ohio. For three days the authors, twenty-three respondents, and a large audience grappled with important issues. Members of the seminary's administration and faculty—especially President John Dickhaut and Professor Roy Reed—as well as members of the Board of Trustees, student body, and secretarial staff worked resourcefully to make that occasion both possible and enjoyable. The investment of mental and physical labor by all who contributed will be amply repaid if this volume stimulates fresh thought about Methodism's ecumenical destiny.

i
the church, ecumenism, and methodism

I have been invited to analyze the relation of Methodism and ecumenism from a non-Methodist point of view. I shall approach this task very indirectly. Two factors have impelled me to do so, one personal, the other sociological. The personal factor is this: I am not a non-Methodist, but an ex-Methodist. There is a difference. For four decades The Methodist Church formed the horizons of my existence. I was shaped by the experiences and disciplines of a Methodist parsonage, Sunday school, and Epworth League, by work in various orchestras and choirs, by training in college and seminary, and by membership in an annual conference. It was as a Methodist, in response to the influence of such professors as Rall and Schermerhorn, that I first became attracted to ecumenical ventures. My mind has changed, of course, since I transferred membership, but, so far as I can tell, I am the same person. Even so, I am an ex-Methodist, and that does make a difference. No woman treats an ex-husband as a non-husband! With me, as with other migrants, it is difficult to avoid distortions of perspective in appraising the former homeland. I will therefore stress the challenges with which ecumenism confronts *all* Protestant denominations, but with special reference to The United Methodist Church.

The sociological factor is even more decisive. The features of American Methodism are common to so many denominations that it is hazardous indeed to prescribe any differentiating marks. Moreover, when one thinks of world Methodism, he soon recognizes that diversities within this family are greater than those which separate it from other Protestant

19

groups. All Methodists, to be sure, trace their ancestry to the same founder. Persistent search may reveal various marks of this common inheritance, yet there is little which distinguishes this family essentially from others.[1] The history of denominations has reached the point where the historian can no longer write a separate biography for each. It is quite futile, therefore, to assume that the two entities *Methodism* and *ecumenism* can be defined with sufficient precision to permit dependable diagrams of their interaction.

Instead of drafting such a diagram, I will ponder three questions: 1) What is the central dilemma in ecclesiological doctrine which must be faced by every denomination? 2) How do current developments in ecumenism bear upon the future both of denominations and councils? 3) What challenges now confront The United Methodist Church, as representative of Protestantism and especially of American Protestantism? Let us consider these three queries in that order.

1. A Dilemma in Ecclesiology

When one reviews various recent efforts to express a Christian understanding of the church, he may well be amazed at the degree of apparent consensus, so long as attention remains focused on the *una sancta* of the Nicene Creed. (Parenthetically, let me say that to avoid semantic confusion, I shall limit the term "church" to this object of faith as

---

[1] I am quite aware of the Methodist assertions of a distinctive witness, as in Par. 6 of the 1968 General Conference "Resolution on The United Methodist Church and the Cause of Christian Unity" (*Daily Christian Advocate,* April 29, 1968, p. 280), but I question the accuracy and significance of these assertions.

expressed in the creeds, using the term "denominations" when referring to those bodies which are members of the World Council of Churches, and employing the term "congregations" in speaking of the separate local units of those various denominations.) A first point of consensus is the insistence upon the trinitarian source and ground for the life of the church. Recall, for example, the opening sentences of an oft-quoted document from the New Delhi Assembly of the World Council: "The love of the Father and the Son in the unity of the Holy Spirit is the source and goal of the unity which the Triune God wills for all men and creation. We believe that we share in this unity in the Church of Jesus Christ." [2]

One finds a similar trinitarian emphasis in the ecclesiological formulations of Vatican II. In Chapter I of *Lumen Gentium (Dogmatic Constitution on the Church)*, for example, the church is viewed in St. Cyprian's words as "a people made one with the unity of the Father, the Son, and the Holy Spirit." [3] So, too, at Uppsala, where Orthodox and Roman Catholic voices exerted a stronger influence on the discussions than ever before, there was a renewed insistence that each of the *notae ecclesiae* should be described in trinitarian terms. Catholicity, for example, should be seen as an expression of the purpose of Christ "to bring people of all times, of all races, of all places, of all conditions, into an or-

[2] *The New Delhi Report: The Third Assembly of the World Council of Churches, 1961,* W. A. Visser 't Hooft, ed. (New York: Association Press, 1962), p. 116. Although one should not exaggerate the authority of an Assembly document, in this case the quotation accurately reflects a wide cross section of ecumenical thought.

[3] *The Documents of Vatican II,* Walter M. Abbott, S. J., ed. (New York: Guild Press, 1966), p. 17.

ganic and living unity in Christ by the Holy Spirit under the universal fatherhood of God."[4] At times insistence on the trinitarian formula became almost ridiculous, as when at the final plenary session at Uppsala, an Orthodox request was granted which modified the closing prayer in the "Message" in such a way as to include a reference to the Holy Spirit. Although the recognition of the Holy Trinity thus can easily become an ecumenical shibboleth, there is no denying the fact that any ecclesiology today, to be acceptable at all, must be firmly grounded in the continuing activity of the Triune God. We cannot otherwise do justice to the church's unity, holiness, catholicity, or apostolicity. This is fully true of the pronouncements of the World Council, even though that body disclaims any intention of advancing "any one particular doctrine" of the church. Much thinking about the church may tacitly deny its divine origins and may adopt a purely sociological orientation.[5] Nevertheless, formal ecumenical pronouncements must embody an explicitly trinitarian ecclesiology.

A second point of consensus is the insistence that in affirming the two basic dimensions of the church (i.e., its divine-human, heavenly-earthly, Adamic-Christic character), the heavenly dimension merits the priority. Quite typical are these words from the Vatican II *Constitution on the Sacred Liturgy:* "In her [the church] the human *is directed and subordinated* [italics mine] to the divine, the visible like-

---

[4] *The Uppsala Report 1968*, Norman Goodall, ed. (Geneva: World Council of Churches, 1968), p. 13.

[5] An example of this implicit positivism may be found in the popular term "superchurch." A trinitarian perception of ecclesial reality would never admit such a term to the vocabulary.

wise to the invisible, action to contemplation, and this present world to that city yet to come." [6]

A third feature of ecumenical ecclesiology emerges as soon as the priority of the divine nature is asserted: the recognition of the difficulties in defining how the "two natures" of the church are precisely related. How can members of the visible earthly church perceive, comprehend, and articulate the multiple connections between the visible and the invisible, the earthly and the heavenly? Theologians from many traditions agree in repudiating an extreme form of the "invisible church" doctrine. They assert that the invisible does become visible. Incarnation is a reality. Docetism has become a theological swearword, all too freely applied to any tendency that a person dislikes. But the problem is not solved by shibboleths, but only by acute vision. How may we perceive the place where the invisible church becomes visible? Where may we locate the roads by which men actually come within the liberating gates of the holy city?

Christian theologians rather quickly reject the two theoretical extremes: on the one hand, a total identification of the invisible and the visible, and on the other, a total disjunction between them. If excessive disjunction has been the Protestant temptation, the temptation of the Roman Catholic and the Eastern Orthodox Churches has been excessive identification. At Vatican II, however, the Catholic Church turned decisively away from this temptation. It did this in its *Constitution on the Church,* when an editorial amendment was approved, a change which in the judgment of some *periti* was the most important single-word change made

* *Documents,* pp. 137-38.

23

in a Vatican II document. In the following paragraph, it was decided to use the verb *subsists in* rather than the verb *is:*

> The society furnished with hierarchical agencies and the Mystical Body of Christ are not to be considered as two realities. . . . Rather they [i. e., "the earthly Church" and the "Church enriched with heavenly things"] form one interlocked reality which is comprised of a divine and a human element. . . . This Church, constituted and organized in the world as a society, *subsists in* [italics mine] the Catholic Church.[7]

The tendency to move away from a total identification of the two realities has, I believe, been gaining momentum since Vatican II among Catholic theologians. This tendency is less noticeable in Orthodox ecclesiology. But what of Protestant thought? Has our ecclesiology been moving away from the earlier disjunction between visible and invisible church?

The New Delhi Assembly indicated a positive answer. In dealing with the subject of unity, for example, the Assembly affirmed the divine reality of the church in an opening paragraph, and then in a second paragraph it declared that this invisible unity "is being made visible." It was wise to shift at this point from nouns to a verb and also to use a verb in the passive voice. This implies that the heavenly reality makes its presence known in action, and in the action of persons who take a common action because they have been acted upon. Apart from the action of a visible community, the divine source of that action does not become visible. Such action becomes visible locally when particular congregations

[7] *Ibid.,* pp. 22-23.

resist multiple corporate inhibitions and inherited habits in order to manifest that unity which has been given to them in Christ. There, to use the idiom of *Lumen Gentium*, the invisible and the visible are interlocked; there the invisible community subsists in the visible. This is true, however, only if the Holy Spirit enables men to recognize the interlocking. It is never self-evident that specific phenomena constitute the decisive points where the invisible reality of the church breaks through into visibility.

It is in the discernment of these points that a relatively new and powerful ecclesiology is now coming to the surface. What appeared first as a nebulous mood is now taking shape as a self-conscious movement. One of the features which is likely to be remembered as distinguishing the Uppsala Assembly is the vigorous exposition of this ecclesiology. Let me outline three components of this ecclesiology which today offer a direct challenge both to conciliarism and to denominationalism.

2. A New Type of Ecumenism

The first component may be called an anti-denominationalist thrust. Please remember that in using the term "denomination" I am referring to the national unit, e.g. The United Methodist Church, in those respects in which it can and does act as a single entity. This unit should be distinguished from the local congregation on the one hand and from the *una sancta* on the other.

That in many members' minds a difference exists among these three has been obvious since the 1957 North American Conference on Faith and Order. In preparing for that conference a commission in New York made a study of the relative strength of the loyalties of members in the congregations on Staten Island. It tried to determine how laymen measure the comparative strength of three loyalties, those to the congregation, to the denomination, and to the church. The commission learned that there was a definite pattern which was remarkably similar in all the "standard" traditions. The strongest loyalty centered on the congregation. Slightly less strong was the loyalty to the church as a universal community. Weakest by far was the loyalty to the denomination. I believe that this disparity has grown larger during the intervening decade.

Let me mention more recent, though more ambiguous, developments. At the 1963 World Conference on Faith and Order, perhaps the greatest frustration was experienced in that subsection which attempted to evaluate the ecclesiological character of councils of churches. An impasse developed between Protestants and Orthodox. The latter generally refused to grant to councils any positive ecclesiological significance whatever, while the former were inclined to grant to the work of the councils a *koinonia*, a *diakonia*, a *leitourgia* which in some respects represented the life and mission of the church in more authentic fashion than the similar work within existing denominations. In the expectations and demands at Uppsala, as expressed by both the student power group and the black power group, this "Protestant" tendency was clearly present, although still somewhat hidden. These groups acted as if the decisions made at Uppsala would more fully represent the mind of the church than would the decisions made either in New York City at 475 Riverside Drive, or in Nashville, Tennessee.

In short, many Christians are far more doubtful of the ecclesiological character of the denomination than of the conciliar forms of Christian community.

Let us illustrate the problem from another angle. Since 1965 two theological commissions have been at work exploring the meaning of catholicity, one group composed of World Council and Roman Catholic theologians, the other of Faith and Order members preparing materials for use at Uppsala. Both commissions found that steady progress was possible as long as they were concerned with describing the *una sancta*. Each theologian believed deeply in the reality of catholicity. Each hungered for a greater receptivity to that catholicity. Accordingly, we managed to draft statements which verbalized a genuine consensus, since we had uncovered a kinship in which there was no place for the abrasiveness of earlier discussions of the *notae ecclesiae*. Yet at the end, in both commissions, it became apparent that we had not even broached the vital question: What is the relationship between the catholicity of the church and the catholicity of our specific denominations, whether The United Methodist Church or the Roman Catholic Church? Had we insisted upon specific answers to that question, a set of joint conclusions would probably have been quite impossible. It is easier to define the catholicity (or unity, holiness, apostolicity) of the church than the catholicity of our own denomination as a denomination.[8] When Protestants ask at what points the invisible holy city becomes visible, they

---

[8] A limited awareness of this factor is indicated in Par. 4 of the resolution already referred to that was adopted by the 1968 General Conference: "We see in none of the existing churches as they now exist the perfect exemplar of the fullness of the Christian community we seek."

seldom answer (unless prompted) by referring to their own denomination. There is, then, a growing reluctance to think of the denomination as the church in a full and true sense.

This first component is related to a second, which may be called "anti-transcendentalism." In many sectors today there is a pronounced and growing allergy toward theological descriptions of the church which give priority to its divine and heavenly ground. Why should this rebellion be so pronounced? Why should it carry so strong a distaste for ecclesiologies that are biblically grounded and dogmatically formulated? No simple answer can do justice to so complex a phenomenon, yet some aspects of this revolt against transcendence are relevant to our problem here. One of the roots of the death-of-God theology is the fact that previous theologies have articulated concepts of God which have inhibited the freedom of man and thus damaged his dignity and creativity. A God imprisoned within human concepts always enslaves men's minds and wills. The emphasis on transcendence may express an attitude toward human existence that is closed and static, expressive of a deterministic view of the past rather than emancipated by an open view of the future. Once a given denomination has established a two-natures ecclesiology, it has readily felt justified in advancing a demonic *non sequitur*. It has appealed to the authority of the Triune God to legitimate its claims to authority over its members. It has defined the visible manifestations of the invisible city in such a way as to inhibit the freedom of those members. Thus it has been able to safeguard its growing wealth, its mystique as a religious and cultural institution, and its power to control its priestly hierarchy. Who can deny that appeals to "the communion of saints" have often been used to support the conservative prejudices of "God's frozen people"? Some denominations have been more guilty of this confusion than others. It is these very denominations which are experiencing the more radical rebellion against transcendence. To some rebels the rejection of ecclesiological transcendence becomes one way of demolishing the credibility of the denomination as an agent of the Eternal. A death-of-the-church theology is thus an important constituent of the death-of-God theology.

There are, of course, other ways to attack denominational idolatries than by denying the doctrine of transcendence. A more direct attack may be mounted against its earthly form as a social institution. A radical anti-institutionalism characterizes much left-wing ecumenism today. A denomination can reply to this attack by appealing to the doctrine of incarnation, but the ecumenical rebels of today reply that the reality of incarnation is one thing, while the identification of the incarnation with a specific set of ecclesiastical structures is quite another. They are inclined to discern the realities of the divine presence, not so much in the defense of Christian institutions as in the attack upon them. Where does one discern the visible signs of an authentic preaching of the Word? "Surely not," they say, "in the standardized, cautious pulpit utterances of a professional ministry, which has been domesticated by ordination and kept under control by promises of salary and annuity. Authentic preaching of the Word is more likely to be heard at a protest rally or a university sit-in." Where should one look today to find the Eucharist rightly administered? At an altar where priest and communicants have slavishly obeyed rubrics which were originally designed to safeguard the exclusive claims of one denomination? Or around a table where fighters against racism or militarism, though drawn from many denominations, have discovered a solidarity more profound than they had previously known?

At Uppsala, the most representative Christian gathering in nine centuries, delegates from America were made aware of the explosive energy of several dissident groups. The first was a youth group which had largely repudiated the structuring of Christian community into the conventional congregational and denominational molds. The second was a black coalition which could see little genuine catholicity in predominantly white denominations because of the presence of white racism, which is no less demonic by being unconscious of its own existence. The third was a group of delegates from the Third World, who discern in denominations of the West many grotesque perversions and distortions of the basic mandate of the church. To some of them, Western denominations are no less paternalistic than Western governments, and no less inclined to hoard their institutional wealth and power, and, what is more important, Western denominations are too confident that they are fully entitled to the term "church."

To sum up, then, we may say that within the ecumenical movement as a whole, and even within the narrower circle of the councils, there is appearing a cluster of radical groups, "God-squads" if you will, who are allergic to denominationalism, transcendentalism, and institutionalism. They are impatient with the slow pace of conciliar processes and with the irrelevance of denominational policies. They enlist eagerly in guerrilla battles against both. Their resistance to existing institutions often is so uncompromising that they seem to have no ecclesiology at all. Yet a positive ecclesiology is often implicit in their rebellion, since they detect the signs of authentic Christian community in events and forces quite distinct from the traditional functions of that community. They raise several inescapable questions:

How do we form a uniting and united church when we may not know *what* the church is? How do we talk so easily about the church when we may not know *where* the church is? What radically new form must the church take if it is to identify itself with a sick society? [9]

The rebels do not readily accept conventional answers to those questions. In fact, they usually intimate that they already know what the church is *not* and where it is *not*. It is *not* to be located in the inherited denominational structures; God has already left those structures behind.

We turn now to the last of our three questions: What challenges now confront the Protestant denominations as represented by The United Methodist Church? We take first the challenges stemming from the projected growth of conciliarism and then those presented by guerrilla or secular ecumenists.

3. Some Challenges to Methodism

What has Methodism contributed since 1910 to the development of conciliarism? We can grant that Methodism has contributed its quota of ecumenical pioneers, its proportionate share in budgetary resources, its contingent of members for theological commissions and council staffs. At few

[9] David C. Myler, "A Student Looks at COCU," *Theology Today*, XXV (1968), 255.

points in recent ecumenical history have Methodists not been present, adding vigor, enthusiasm, and imagination to common enterprises. I am not disposed to scoff at such contributions. Yet for the sake of proportion and accuracy, we must quench the euphoria which accompanies such observations by asking blunt questions. What, for example, have been the relative degrees of growth in conciliar and Methodist structures?

In the period when councils have been making quite spectacular gains, American Protestant denominations, and Methodism in particular, have been gaining institutional momentum at an even greater rate. The extent of growth in centralized power and affluence on the part of this denomination is amazing. I am not speaking alone of statistics of church membership and attendance (though even there I find the growth impressive), but of the proliferation of bureaus, offices, staffs, and of the budgetary provisions to support the central agencies and to maintain the connectional system. The power and size of the denominational structure have never been greater. Compared to the budget and staff of the World Council of Churches, the Methodist institution is mammoth and becoming more mammoth by leaps and bounds, illustrating several of the laws of Mr. Parkinson. If one's actions are to be dominated by fear of great monolithic institutions, then it is quite ridiculous for a Methodist to be afraid either of the World Council or of the Consultation on Church Union.

It is also instructive to observe the differences in status accorded to those who staff denominational or ecumenical enterprises. Granted that election to the staff of a council may carry a degree of glamor and that the staff person himself may feel excitement in being where the action is, a Methodist will almost certainly gain greater professional advantage by channeling his energies into causes which leave a mark on annual conference reports, which involve close cooperation with district superintendents and bishops, and which strengthen his ties with fellow Methodists. A term of service with any interdenominational enterprise (council, seminary, journal, inner-city project) usually damages those connections which form the basis of rising expectations. For corroboration, ask almost any Methodist who has served outside a strictly Methodist institution. It is difficult, of course, to measure the disparity between the rewards for denominational and for ecumenical work, but it seems to me that the gap is steadily growing, if one measures the issue, as many Methodists do, by the list of those elected to the episcopacy.

One needs also to appraise the degree of authority which has been assigned to conciliar enterprises. Never has verbal commitment to ecumenism been greater; never has the relaxation of autonomy been less. It is the denominations which have devised and approved the rules for the conciliar game. These rules have explicitly excluded any grant of ecclesial authority.[10] Membership in councils has abridged the sovereignty of denominations no more than membership in the U.N. has abridged the sovereignty of nations. Councils speak to the denominations, not for them.

Councils voluntarily abjure all claims to being the church; they do not require that their members should recognize

[10] This was explicitly recognized at the recent General Conference at Dallas: "No council has any immediate jurisdiction in any of our own affairs" (*Daily Christian Advocate*, p. 317). As long as this is true the affirmations of support carry little substantive weight.

other members as churches. The World Council does not even require that its members subscribe to its budget, a privilege of which several dozen members take advantage. Every conciliar appointment must (at least in principle) be approved by the appointee's denomination. Even when a denomination appoints delegates to a World Council Assembly, no authority is given them to commit their denomination to anything. Ask anyone who was a delegate both to the Dallas General Conference and to the Uppsala Assembly. Appointment to the latter may have carried greater honor, but it surely carried less governing authority. The challenges of conciliarism to denominationalism can be kept under moderate control as long as the policy decisions of councils are made by committees composed in large part of executives of the denominations.

This does not mean that these challenges are nonexistent but rather that they operate indirectly and subtly. For example, Faith and Order discussions of the *notae ecclesiae*, as we have already noticed, no longer assume that denominational structures have an essential role in ecclesiology. Or in the realm of social policy, problems like racism confront the denominations with the irrelevance of their own separateness when it comes to influencing society. Or in the realm of missions, the work of councils demonstrates the efficacy, even the necessity, of joint action if denominational objectives are to be realized. There is a steady escalation of pressures, encouraged by the councils, which makes it less and less possible for any denomination to go it alone. So steady is the momentum away from isolation that there is ample reason for isolationists to take alarm and to build up various defenses.

Among the defense mechanisms is one that can be noticed in much Methodist promotional literature: an increasing tendency to rely upon the reiteration of the adjective "Methodist." Often the appeal to the label assumes a certain ultimate value in being a Methodist. It implies that one of the strongest motives of members is the desire to become a better Methodist. It reflects, at least on the part of writers, a strong reliance upon the existence of a Methodist mystique. When this adjective appears so much more frequently than the adjective "Christian," the outsider is led to wonder whether this is actually the primary element in the self-identity of this community. Or is it rather the accepted stock-in-trade of professional bell ringers? Every denomination needs to become more aware of such defense mechanisms.

The more sophisticated method of defending the autonomy of the denomination vis-à-vis the councils is to stress the ecclesiological deficiencies of the latter. A council does not celebrate the sacraments, preach the gospel, or ordain ministers. Such actions fall under the exclusive jurisdiction of some denomination. It matters not that the *notae ecclesiae* may be seen more clearly in the work of the council. What matters is the authoritative administration of Word and sacraments, and this fact insures the denomination its status. As a matter of fact, a denomination as such neither preaches nor celebrates. Those actions take place within a congregation. The denomination's control is exercised by way of its control of ordained ministers. In spite of the recognition of ministers from other churches, which ecumenical courtesy virtually demands, few changes have yet occurred in the juridical rubrics by which a denomination maintains its own clerical identity. Each denomination is in fact a labor union that has established a closed shop. The denomination determines the requirements for membership and conducts the proceedings of initiation; it establishes salary scales and exerts control over a man's advancement from one echelon to another; it demands a regular reporting of work done, with the power of annual review; it can give or remove certification of good standing; it can assure or threaten the security of a man before and after retirement; in some cases, as in Methodism, every appointment must be renewed every year. It is not surprising that if church union schemes founder, they founder on the plans for unifying ministries. For it is in this area that the practical sovereignty of a particular denominational establishment is threatened.

The conciliar challenges to the denomination cannot get out of hand as long as denominational executives belong to the governing committees of the councils. But what is impossible for the conciliar agency becomes quite possible for the guerrilla ecumenist. He can and often does deny the authority of the denomination to determine the validity of preaching, sacraments, and ministerial orders. So we must now turn to see how this more radical challenge confronts The United Methodist Church.

Under the memorial to John and Charles Wesley in Westminster Abbey are the words: "God buries his workmen but carries on his work." This principle is undoubtedly true. It can also be extended a step: "God buries not only his workmen but also the forms of his (and their) work." In the case of the two Wesleys, this can be seen in the emergence of a separate denomination, in the proliferation of that denomination into a large family of denominations, and in the submerging of the denomination in various church unions of the twentieth century. Are we now watching a further metamorphosis? There are many analysts and activists today, who have been dubbed "anonymous ecumenists," who believe that in his good providence God is about to "bury" both the denominations and the conciliar movement. As transient devices for structuring the life of the Christian community, both have made significant contributions, but both have become obsolete. The wind of the Holy Spirit is now choosing to blow in directions away from the traditional structures of both denominations and councils.

It is easy for "ecclesiastical squares" to misjudge the motives for this form of ecumenism. This is not simply a reversion to radical individualism inasmuch as these people are usually drawn into tightly knit cadres of action, where the degree of mutual concern is greater than they have earlier known. Nor is it a new form of perfectionism, since many of them are fully aware of the power of sin to corrupt even the best causes. Nor is this a blatant form of secularized humanism, for these activists are frequently conscious of the presence of God in the world and are fully committed to finding Christ among the least of his brethren. There is an implicit ecclesiology undergirding their protests which actually holds quite close to traditional lines. "The church is to be found where the gospel is rightly proclaimed." Yes. But where do they find such a gospel? Where disciples of Christ have broken radically with the principalities and powers that govern those religious institutions which are subsidized and therefore controlled by a corrupted society. "The church is to be found where the sacraments are rightly celebrated." Yes. But where do they find such a celebration? On the battle lines, among the sit-ins, in ghetto homes, wherever

Christ's love has riveted together a band of his soldiers. An appropriate celebration is found where men and women ignore or defy denominational traditions and inhibitions, and break a loaf of bread together. Here they discover *koinonia* in Christ. The Hallelujahs and the Amens, as well as the sermons and sacraments, are no longer the monopoly of clergymen bound by denominational discipline. Effective government depends on the consent of the governed, and many of the most devoted servants of Christ have now withdrawn that consent from the various echelons of ecclesiastical authority. At least there is a rapidly increasing number of dropouts, who, like Charles Davis, deplore the absence of the authentic marks of the church from both Catholic and Protestant bodies and who find them present only "where Christian faith, love, and hope are both possible and actual." [11] There are no doubt thousands of American Protestants who no longer view the Christian vocation as dependent on membership in a denomination.

If we ask what is the destiny of Methodism in an ecumenical age, and if we take this type of guerrilla ecumenism as prophetic of what lies ahead, the only valid answer is that Methodism has no future in such an age, that is, no future *as Methodism*. The denominational form of organization cannot thrive long after devoted men dissociate loyalty to Christ from loyalty to that form. All denominations become vulnerable to the attacks of these God-squads which, in response to the presumed guidance of the Holy Spirit and in conscious allegiance to the Christ of the New Testament, are brazen enough to formulate ecclesiological doctrine in such

[11] William Hamilton, review of Charles Davis' A *Question of Conscience*, in *Theology Today*, XXV (1968), 265.

a way as to demythologize denominational claims, and courageous enough to develop modes of action in the world which enable men to see the *una sancta* as present in the secular world, yet quite remote from the practices and pieties of traditional denominations.

Consider, by way of illustration, how many men have recently revised their ecclesiology as a result of sharing in the struggle for racial equality. In this new Reformation, in which an American Martin Luther was prophet and saint, they have seen convincing signs of that ministry, that preaching, that fellowship, and those sacraments which authentically mark the life of the people of God. To be sure, Dr. King was a Baptist, a minister, a supporter of official ecumenism; yet he and thousands of his disciples discovered in civil rights and pacifist agitation a mode of community life for which denominational forms were irrelevant. Of these disciples, many will never again think of themselves primarily as Methodists, because the primary community to which they now belong has made obsolete all traditional labels except that of Christian.

Does Methodism contribute to this form of ecumenism? I believe it does, and especially in two ways. For one thing, the power of the guerrillas stems in part from their crusading idealism, their romantic activism, their hope for new messiahs. I believe that no denomination has more effectively contributed to this mood than has the Methodist (consider, for example, the popularity of "Rise up, O men of God" and "Are ye able?"). For another thing, the power of the guerrillas grows in proportion to the effort of the establishment to restrain them and to control them. Any effort to exercise discipline over them succeeds only in fanning the flames of rebellion. I believe that no Protestant denomination has provided a better bellows than the Methodist. Herein lies one of the ironies of the present situation: the very process by which denominations enhance their power creates the conditions which make rebellion all the more certain and all the more explosive. If today one asks where the sense of belonging to the one church is strongest, he must consider as a possible answer: "There where rebels gather from all the denominations."

I do not wish to defend or to glorify current rebellions against denominational institutions, but I believe that we must listen at least to the kind of definition they are giving to the church. Is it true or false that the holiness of the church becomes especially visible today among such agencies as the Southern Christian Leadership Conference? That the church's apostolicity becomes visible where the mission to the secular world is taken most seriously? That her unity becomes visible where loyalty to Christ produces corporate acts of rebellion like those against the Vietnam War? That her catholicity becomes most visible outside the routine operations of the congregation and the denomination? Where, how, and by whom is the gospel of Jesus Christ being most faithfully proclaimed? Where and how is his body being knit together by his Eucharist?

Behind these questions lurks a single basic issue. Is the denomination as such entitled to claim the name *church* in the strongest sense of that name? It would be much easier for those national administrative entities to justify their existence if they did not advance this claim. The chief merit of anonymous ecumenism is the articulation of this challenge, and there is much to be said for it. We have too quickly and too easily forgotten the sound theological reasons which in the past impelled many Christians to deny the term "church" to these administrative entities. Those theological arguments were overridden more on pragmatic grounds and on grounds of linguistic habit than for convincing theological reasons.

Although I cannot here argue the case, let me remind you of several arguments which have by no means lost their cogency. There is, for instance, no scriptural ground or warrant for calling our denominations churches. Moreover, it becomes increasingly difficult for the historian to link a particular denomination to the biblical images of the people of God (e.g. the body of Christ), to the key phrases in the creeds and confessions (e.g. the communion of saints), and to the *notae ecclesiae,* whether we choose the multiple signs of the New Testament, the four adjectives of the Nicene Creed, or those subtle evidences which emerge in the pluralistic society of today. The significant ecclesiological documents in recent ecumenical history, whether enunciated at New Delhi, Rome, Montreal, or Uppsala, are those in which the church is described in terms which cannot be readily applied to the denominations as such.

Denominations are usually national entities. The church is not. Denominations are strictly post-Reformation Western sociological phenomena. The church is not. Denominations as institutional structures are patterned after cultural and political models and carry on their work in ways set by nonreligious institutions. The church does not. Denominations, as a result of homogenization within a common culture, develop similar programs and adopt similar patterns of organization, so that their original distinctiveness fades out and

41

their original claims to separate existence lose their force. This is not true of the church. Denominations now find it impossible to speak on current problems with a single voice, or to make ethical decisions as a single agent, or to exercise discipline over their members. The church is recognized by the fact that it does so speak, act, and suffer, whether in Watts, on Wall Street, or in a Boston courtroom.

Part of the difficulty here is semantic. Few important terms carry such an endless range of denotations and connotations as the term "church." But it compounds the confusion of trivial with profound meanings to apply this term to such organizations as have their headquarters at 475 Riverside Drive. The term has lost its power to indicate clearly what these organizations actually do, in distinction from what the church of Christ actually does. A denomination, in function and operation, has actually become an administrative agency for linking congregations together (congregations which in themselves are composed of Christians of diverse denominational backgrounds and beliefs), for assisting those congregations in their local work, for channeling their participation in national and international enterprises, for providing them with accredited ministers, and for providing those ministers with vocational mobility and security. There are historical and pragmatic reasons why the term "church" should be applied to such an agency, but are there adequate theological reasons?

I believe that the progress of ecumenical ecclesiology has posed this question, that the dependence of the councils on the denominations has prevented them from pressing it, and that rebellious ecumenism has forced both the councils and the denominations to take that question with utmost seriousness. In modern society, all churches (not excluding the Orthodox or the Catholic) have become denominations, *de facto* if not *de jure*. Perhaps in an age that will be truly ecumenical it will be the destiny of all denominations to decrease so that the church may increase. If so, we should stop thinking of the denomination as church. But before that happens, a revolution must take place which is far greater than even our most radical rebels have conceived. The ultimate question is whether the Christ whom we meet in the Gospels, in the sacraments, in the creeds, in the new age— whether this Jesus who is Lord of the church because he is first Lord of all being—whether he demands such a revolution and whether through the Holy Spirit he will empower it. The ecumenical age has just begun. None of us can yet predict its ultimate impact on those denominations which for better and worse we call churches. In this regard we are like the European map makers who in 1650 were attempting to map the North American continent.

43

ii
methodism's theological heritage: a study in perspective

Even in a revolutionary age, the past is still prelude to the future. What is more, our freedom for that future depends at least partly on our present self-understanding in the light of our traditions and corporate experience, since these control our perspectives. In the case of a historical entity like Methodism, any realistic look ahead demands a careful retrospect: a synoptic view of the theological past that we share with all other Christians and an identification of those distinctive emphases, if any, that we may call our own.

In any such essay in perspective, the Methodist ecumenist had best walk warily. On his right is the gaping pit of denominational triumphalism with its claim that the Methodists constitute a doctrinal species all their own, with some sort of divine right and duty to defend their differences to the death. Such a claim is doubly false, as a matter of fact and as a matter of ecumenical principle. Directly on the left, however, is the miry swamp of doctrinal indifferentism—the blinkered assertion that Methodists have no unique doctrinal contribution to offer the whole church, that *all* our concerns are practical, missional, social. This, too, is false, in fact and on principle—and the principle has a significant bearing on our ecumenical involvement. Speak as ardently as you will of the primacy of mission over doctrine (in my view, a wholly gratuitous disjunction), and it is still true that *the Christian message is the Christian mission* and that the measure of mission is not mission itself but rather *the hearing of faith* (cf. Rom. 10:17). If it is true, as I hope to show, that the Methodists have, or had, a distinctive understanding of what goes into "the hearing of faith," then it would follow that our particular understanding of that message affects our understanding of the Christian mission. And if it is also true, as I have argued for thirty years, that it is Methodism's manifest destiny to lose its denominational life in a more vital, catholic community of Christians ("that the world may believe"), then it will matter immensely if we can make our "death" truly meaningful: an offertory of our best gifts to the wider union —and I keep hoping that this will include our intellects along with our hearts and muscle!

This is why, therefore, I make bold to propose a bare-bones sketch of the thesis that Wesleyan Methodism has a unique and identifiable doctrinal emphasis of considerable import both for mission *and* ecumenism; that this "doctrinal emphasis" does not add up to a singular *system* of doctrine, whole and entire, but is rather a delicate balance of emphases and accents which is all too often out of kilter but which remains relevant for our part in the ecumenical dialogue. In short, Methodist doctrine has a distinctive style of integrating the evangelical stress on God's sovereign grace and the catholic accent on man's agency in the history of his salvation. There may be nothing very original about the several elements in Methodism's doctrinal stance, but the way they were put together and have been held together *is* unique—and so also the way in which they have been allowed to fall apart!

One graphic way of seeing this point about the difference between separate theological *systems* and unique *configurations* of doctrine is to run a simple experiment in ecumenical cartography. Take any of the theological "maps" in common use and try to locate Methodism on it. The most obvious feature on any of these maps is the great divide between the Catholics (Orthodox and Roman) and the Protestants, and it will scarcely occur to anyone to put the Methodists "over there," on the Catholic side, despite the fact that Wesley was an Anglican, was often denounced as a "papist" and openly avowed his indebtedness to Catholic spirituality. Over on the Protestant side, there is first of all the Lutheran domain, with no place for us there, either—despite our joint professions of loyalty to the *sola scriptura* and *sola fide*. Alongside them is the broader expanse of Calvinist territory (embracing important client groups like the Baptists and the Campbellites), but we don't really "fit" there—despite Wesley's affinities with some elements of the Puritan tradition.[1] Ever since Wesley denounced Whitefield (1739) for preaching "the decrees," the battle between sovereignty and agency has been joined, much mellowed of late, but not at all forgotten.

Then there are the scattered enclaves of the Protestant Radicals who, once penned up, have since scattered abroad and, in America more than elsewhere, have deeply affected their neighbors in matters of ecclesiastical polity. Methodists have deep affinities with Radical Protestantism. We, too, began as a religious society, We, too, have our martyrs and self-righteous memories of having been put upon by the high and the mighty. We, too, set great store by "heart-religion," "the community of the Spirit," "we-group fellowship," and the like. But in England we grew up inside a national church, and in America we grew into an "establish-

---

[1] Cf. Robert C. Monk, *John Wesley: His Puritan Heritage* (Nashville: Abingdon Press, 1966).

ment" of our own—with our "connectional system" as a hallmark of our identity. Besides, many of the Radicals tended to construe Christian experience in mystical terms which offended Wesley mightily.[2]

This leaves us, then, with only one remaining segment on our map—inscribed *Ecclesia Anglicana*—and both we and they shrink from our being spotted *there*. We were never welcome in our homeland, and two centuries of schism have complicated our relationships of affiliation and disaffiliation. We began as a religious society within the Church of England, never more than tolerated. Wesley tried to hold his societies inside the church,[3] except for the Americans whom, finally, he had to consign to the vagaries of a strange providence.[4] But the Wesleyan style of evangelism was discordant in the Church of England, and the Methodist understanding of ministry and the sacraments antipathetic. In the resultant love-hate relationship that developed, the Anglicans lost their most forceful "evangelical" party and the Methodists forfeited their original "catholic" context.

If, then, we are not Catholic in any formal sense, or Lutheran, Calvinist, or Radical, what on earth are we, theologically? Here we ourselves have added to the confusion. To begin with, we accepted the Lutheran and Calvinist view that theology is and ought to be speculative and systematic (albeit biblical, of course): the heroic attempt to discover, expound, and defend that one true *system* of Christian truth

[2] Cf. *The Journal of the Rev. John Wesley, A.M.*, Nehemiah Curnock, ed. (London: Epworth Press, 1911), I, 420 (January 24, 1738).

[3] Cf. *Reasons Against a Separation from the Church of England* (London, 1758); see also *A Preservative Against Unsettled Notions in Religion*, #13 (Bristol, 1758).

[4] Cf. *The Letters of the Rev. John Wesley, A.M.*, John Telford, ed. (London: Epworth Press, 1931), VII, 238-39 (September 10, 1784).

that *must* be lodged somewhere in Scripture and tradition, and to do this by means of abstract conceptualizations ordered into a comprehensive whole. But then we backed away, as if by instinct, from any such enterprise so described.[5] As a result, we have tended to discourage (and to denigrate) theological speculation and scholarship at any level much beyond that of practical utility. Then, in an obvious compensatory reaction, we proceeded to develop a positive pride in our lack of theological prowess.

Meanwhile, what with the nagging of the Calvinists, we adopted as our own their pejorative label for us: "Arminian." This has been doubly confusing. It suggests that Arminius must have been one of Wesley's major sources—and therefore ours—and it implies that Methodism may accurately be classified as a subspecies of aberrant Calvinism (which was Dort's verdict on Arminianism). Both of these implications are false.

It has, therefore, been "doing what comes naturally" for Methodism to evolve through two centuries with a minimal *theological* self-consciousness. Her spokesmen usually have been content to emphasize such particular accents as "religious experience," "assurance," "holiness," and the like, and they opposed various contrary views and practices in other traditions (formalism, predestination, believers' baptism, etc.). But they stopped short of claiming that the Meth-

---

[5] This is what Wesley meant by "orthodoxy" and why he denied to it any normative authority. "Orthodoxy, or right opinions, is, at best, but a very slender part of religion, if it can be allowed to be any part at all." *The Works of John Wesley* (Grand Rapids: Zondervan Publishing House; reprinted from the English authorized edition of 1872), VIII, 249. "As to all opinions which do not strike at the root of Christianity, we think and let think." *Works,* VIII, 340.

odist position amounted to more than a peculiar *configuration* of common Christian doctrine. Latterly, however, this lack of a distinctive theological self-identity has prompted patterns of borrowing from other doctrinal traditions and fashions, especially from European Protestantism (Lotze, Ritschl, Barth, Bultmann). For the most part, however, these transplants were not wholly successful—partly because of a native streak of anthropological doctrine that is characteristic of Wesley and the Anglicans, which produces an emphasis that is not easily understood or explained in the terms of the classical Protestant syndromes. There is a problem here that deserves our careful pondering. It bears on the fact—or what I take to be the fact—that Methodism's share in the history of theology has yet to match its true potential. If we are to improve our record in the future, we had best try harder to understand our past.

Let me suggest, therefore, that Methodist theology, generally speaking, may best be understood as a peculiar brand of evangelical Christianity, with origins in a catholic environment and with its evolution (especially in America) within the milieu of modern secularism. Its most distinctive theological characteristic has been its doctrine of God's grace (the active presence of his love in human existence) in which the prime concern is a vital synthesis of the evangelical stress on God's sovereignty and the catholic emphasis on human agency: a dynamic mix of prevenience, justification, regeneration, and holiness. In other words, when Methodists talk about the ancient paradox of God's ways with men, they have their own recognizable way of trying to explain it all.

This way turns on a notion that has its roots in biblical thought and also a long history down through the unfolding

of Christian doctrine. It is an unstable idea; and it has
generated a teetering effort to keep to the twisting ridge that
runs between the lowlands of moralism and what Wesley
called "solifidianism." [6] It would take a whole book to spell
this out with anything close to adequate argument and docu-
mentation—a book not yet written, and one that may never
be. But some of the landmarks of that history are reasonably
clear, and they do add up to what I hope may be a useful
comment on the future of theology in the Methodist tradition in an ecumenical age.

Christianity is a gospel: about God and man, and about
Jesus as God's special agent in the drama of man's salvation.
It presupposes a radical defect in the human condition and
thereby poses a subtle question about the residual capacities
of "fallen man" within the order and purposes of God's
grace in his ongoing creation. In their perennial wrestlings
with these questions, Christians have turned up a genuine
paradox: God's undisputed sovereignty *and* man's undeniable
responsibility. In every system of Christian doctrine, God's
sovereignty is asserted or assumed; there are no humanists
in Holy Writ nor in the company of the church's accredited
teachers. And yet also and equally, there is the recognition
of human agency as decisive in the mysteries of both sin and
redemption. From the J story of Yahweh and Adam in their
first unequal confrontation (Gen. 3:9-23) down to the Reve-
lator's vision of "a new heaven and a new earth" (Rev. 22),
there runs the insistent theme of God's prevenient and prevailing grace, in the sustenance of his creation and in his
"providence" for his rebellious creatures. "For it is by *his*
grace you are saved, through trusting him; it is *not* your own

---

[6] Cf. *Journal*, II, 174; see also V, 244.

doing. It is God's *gift*, not a reward for work done" (Eph. 2:8 NEB, italics added). And yet the human share in this process is utterly crucial. Salvation is an interpersonal affair. The human condition is ruinous, and yet its residual *dignitas* prompted God to give us freely his costing love in Jesus Christ. It is God, of course, who works in aid of all our willings and doings; *all* our powers are created, and he is their Creator and Sustainer. And yet their God-chosen purpose is to involve us deeply in holy history, to *work out our own salvation*, with fear and trembling (cf. Phil. 2:12).

Through crisis after crisis this paradox has persisted, and Christians have dealt with it in as many different ways as they could conceive. In the East, the tendency was to stress God's image in man, spoiled by sin but not negated—man's capacity for participation in the divine perfections.[7] All of this was based on the assumption that grace is onmipresent in creation ("a sacramental universe"); hence, the normal mode of faith's appropriation of grace is worship and communion. In Orthodoxy, the chief business of man is *leitourgia* (worship in its broadest and deepest sense); his chief end is *teleōsis* ("perfection," "the fullness of the human possibility").

In the West, the Pelagian controversy polarized the Christian mind and moved Latin orthodoxy over to a one-sided emphasis on the gratuity of grace. The unhappiest consequence of that tragedy was the strength it gave to the notion that *any* version of divine-human synergism could easily be smeared by calling it "Pelagian." The Second Council of

---

[7] Cf. David L. Balás, *Methousia Theou; Man's Participation in God's Perfections According to Saint Gregory of Nyssa* (Rome: Libreria Herder, 1966), and Lars Thunberg, *Microcosm and Mediator: The Theological Anthropology of Maximus the Confessor* (Lund: C. W. K. Gleerup, 1965).

Orange (529) and Boniface II (531) proceeded to confer semi-dogmatic status upon the triumphant Augustinianism that had emerged from the ruins of the Roman Empire. But what of man's "natural" capacity for grace, if any? What happens, or can happen, in the human heart in the way of preparing it for "the hearing of faith"? This was a question of great urgency and moment in the church's missionary ventures in a barbaric society. It makes a great deal of difference how you preach to the unconverted whether you assume or reject the premise of God's grace as prevenient, preparatory, and morally active in human existence, always and everywhere.

It was in such a missional context that there emerged in the sixth and seventh centuries a maxim for Christian missionaries that modified the prevailing Augustinianism: *Facienti quod in se est, Deus non denegat gratiam* (God does not withhold his grace from the man who is doing what is truly "him"—*in se*—or as the current phrase has it, "doing his own thing").[8] The expression was a coinage of biblical and patristic sentiments, and in its earliest usage (before Anselm) it referred exclusively to the purely natural human activity (*in se*) that disposed the soul toward justification proper (*gratia infusa*). The power that enabled man to do anything positively by himself (*in se*) was the grace of creation (*concursus Dei,*) one of the functions of which was the preparation of the human will (*habilitas passiva*) that normally precedes the gift and reception of saving grace itself. Is not the man who opens a window to let in the sunshine respon-

---

[8] Cf. A. M. Landgraf, *Dogmengeschichte der Frühscholastik* (Regensburg, 1952-54), I/1, 249-63. See also H. A. Oberman, *The Harvest of Medieval Theology* (Cambridge: Harvard University Press, 1963), pp. 132-45.

sible in some sense for lighting the room, even if he is not responsible for the sunshine?[9] There is no such thing as saving grace (*meritum de condigno*) in human virtue, but there is a sort of "congruent merit" that goes with the *facere in se est.*

This was a way of urging that human nature, even at its worst, is never wholly bereft of grace.[10] Sin has spoiled but not effaced the *imago Dei.* Even in its alienation, the human heart is being stirred and drawn by the immanent action of God's Spirit. Man can, and must, do what he can in response to these promptings and leadings—and God will "pre-vent" (go before) him in love and promise.

This, of course, takes human agency for granted—and thus falls athwart the Augustinian view of what the human *in se* actually is. In those terms, *in se* means depravity and self-deceiving pride. Any virtuous operation of a sinful man's *in se* can issue only in *vitiae splendidae,* "splendid sins." [11]

As Europe began to come of age (in the twelfth century), there gradually arose a new "naturalism"—a spin-off from the revolutions in science, technology, and philosophy that accompanied the importation of Arabic-Aristotelian "secularism" into the collapsing feudal society that had never been more than half-converted. The resulting collision of cultures and world views set off the profoundest crisis of the Middle Ages, with repercussions that still echo in our own bemused ears. The controversy (miscalled "Averroistic") was fought on the highest level of abstractions: the eternity of the world

[9] Cf. Landgraf, *Dogmengeschichte,* pp. 258-59.
[10] Cf. George Matheson's familiar hymn, "O Love that wilt not let me go," and St. Thomas' famous maxim, *gratia non tollit naturam, sed perfecit.*
[11] Cf. *John Wesley,* Albert C. Outler, ed., "A Library of Protestant Thought" (New York: Oxford University Press, 1964), pp. 150, 440.

and matter, the unicity of the intellect, the mortality of the soul, etc. But at urgent issue were the distillates of two rival life-styles: the transcendentalism of "traditional" Christianity and the basic naturalism of "the new philosophy." It was the special vocation of Thomas Aquinas to absorb the full force of this secularizing challenge—so powerful that it fascinated both the intelligentsia and the rising bourgeoisie—and to convert the otherworldly traditions of early medieval Christianity into a new "theologically founded worldliness," in Josef Pieper's interesting phrase.[12] A vital element in this Thomistic synthesis of nature and grace was the premise of the *facienti quod in se est*.[13]

But the immobilists were panicked by the threat of this new secularism. Three years to the day from Thomas' death, "Averroism" was roundly condemned by the Archbishop of Paris in an indictment that also contained several key propositions that had been affirmed by Thomas himself. This suppression was instigated and approved by Pope John XXI and was quickly followed by an even more explicit anti-Thomist condemnation by the Archbishop of Canterbury. Together, they amounted to a powerful attack on the universities of Paris and Oxford, where the new naturalism was rampant. They also had the effect of tainting the reputation of the *Doctor Angelicus*. The cause of Christian naturalism went under a cloud. The next move was up to the transcendentalists.

Presently, then, with Duns Scotus and the nominalists, a new theological compound begins to emerge: radical empiri-

---

[12] Josef Pieper, *Guide to Thomas Aquinas* (New York: Mentor-Omega Books, 1962), p. 117; cf. pp. 118-19.
[13] Cf. *De Veritate*, Q. 28, arts. v-viii. English translation: *Truth* (Chicago: Henry Regnery Company, 1954), III, 380-96.

cism (in logic) in support of radical transcendence (in theology). For the nominalists, reason is reliable only within the
narrowest limits. Faith is able to soar above these limits and
to mark out the distinctions between the twin manifestations
of God's freedom: his *potentia absoluta* and his *potentia
ordinata*. His sovereignty was indicated by the *potentia absoluta*; his *self*-limitations were signified by the *potentia
ordinata*. Thus, human agency reappears in nominalism in a
strange and curious way. As Professor Oberman has explained
it in his excellent *Harvest of Medieval Theology*, the nominalists (and especially Gabriel Biel, Luther's mentor in philosophy) held both divine sovereignty and human agency in
desperate balance—allowing for the congruent merit of man's
natural love of God was a significant preparation for the
condign merit of God's saving grace (God's unmerited gift)—
and the key to this nominalist synthesis was the *facere quod
in se est!* [14] This was an unstable mixture of a radical super-
naturalism and a moderate moralism—yet it also had a very
special relevance to the then current issues of social and
political conflict between the papacy and the empire.

Now there are two points that make all this obscure history relevant to our present theme. The first is that it was
nominalism that Luther and Calvin learned and rejected as
the only philosophy worth learning and rejecting. Indeed,
both the *sola scriptura* and the anti-naturalism of the great
Reformers derive in important measure from their ambivalent
reactions to this particular philosophic outlook. They took
over its transcendental theology; they rejected its humanist
anthropology outright and vehemently. Luther's violent aver-
sions to "natural" theology and morality were stirred by the

[14] Cf. Oberman, *op. cit.*, pp. 120-45.

dangers he saw specifically in the *facere in se est*. Compare his *Disputation Against Scholastic Theology* (September 4, 151), especially Theses #6, 10, 15, 26, 28, 33, 61, 88, 91, 97,[15] together with his attack upon Erasmus in *The Bondage of the Will* (1525), and you can recognize Luther's radical aversion to synergism of every sort. Then, in Calvin's contention (*Institutes*, Book I), that apart from *saving* grace the human will is at odds with God by "nature," that the human mind is (*in se*) an inveterate idol factory, one may see the climactic rejection of the *facere in se est* in classical Protestantism. Thereafter, no version of divine-human synergism would have a welcome place among the strict Lutherans or Calvinists.

The second point that touches us is that the nominalist cause, lost in Protestant Europe, survived in England, and combined with the spirit and substance of the Erasmian reform program to supply the Anglican Reformation with its most distinctive theology. Nominalism had deep roots in England and especially in Oxford. Scotus was an Oxford man; his major work is aptly titled *Opus Oxoniense*. Ockham was trained at Oxford, and four of the five identifiable targets of Thomas Bradwardine's *De causa Dei contra Pelagium* were English and Oxonian.[16] As a philosophy, nominalism was the fibrous root of what became "British empiricism" (Bacon *et seq.*); its theological residues fertilized the special brand

---

[15] Thesis #26: "An act of love is not the best way of doing 'what in one lies.' . . . Nor is it a method of repenting and drawing near to God." Thesis #33: "And that is a false dictum, too, which alleges that to do 'all that in one lies' is to remove the obstacles to grace (against certain teachers)." *Luther: Early Theological Works*, James Atkinson, ed., "Library of Christian Classics" (Philadelphia: Westminster Press, 1962), XVI, 266-73.

[16] Cf. Gordon Leff, *Bradwardine and the Pelagians* (Cambridge: Cambridge University Press, 1957).

of "faith *and* good works" that became the hallmark of the central Anglican tradition in which John Wesley's mind was formed.

All this suggests, and this is the nerve of my thesis, that there was a native-born tradition of Christian synergism in Europe and England long before Arminius and the Synod of Dort—and that it was *this* tradition that nourished Wesley. Such a thesis had already been put forward by a historian whom Wesley read: Peter Heylin in his *Historia Quinquarticularis* (1660). Against the Puritans, Heylin rejected the label "Arminian" as a designation for Anglican theology, on the ground that the Church of England never had been Calvinist. Since "Arminian" denotes an aberrant version of Calvinism, it is a misnomer when applied to *Ecclesia Anglicana.* Heylin makes a correlative point, too: that, beyond its own native traditions, the Church of England owed its foreign debts mainly to Erasmus, Melanchthon, and Bucer. It was neither Lutheran nor Calvinist.[17]

There is no denying that Heylin's history overall is partisan and tendentious, but on these two points he had a good case. The two great charters of "central Anglicanism" had already been drafted before Arminius and Dort—in the Edwardian *Homilies* (1547) and in Richard Hooker's *Laws of Ecclesiastical Polity* (1594-97). In both of these the Methodist reader will recognize a familiar version of the Great Paradox, an argument based on scriptural grounds as decisive in all questions theological, that original sin does not obliterate the *imago Dei,* that salvation is God's gift "with no merit thereunto antecedent," that good works follow justi-

---

[17] Cf. *The Historical and Miscellaneous Tracts of the Rev. and Learned Peter Heylin, D.D.* (London, 1681), pp. 505-634.

fication, and yet that human cooperation is decisive with the whole process: preparation, reception, and harvest. The medieval maxim (*facere in se est*) is not repeated verbatim; its presence as premise is everywhere.

Elsewhere I have tried to indicate the ways in which Wesley, across a lifetime, sought and found a way between the equally unacceptable extremes of moralism and "solifidianism"; how he maintained a rigorist doctrine of original sin along with a generous conception of prevenient grace; how he correlated and distinguished justification, regeneration, and sanctification; how he stood off antinomianism of every kind; how he championed the cause of universal redemption.[18] On justification, he found "not a hair's breadth" of difference with Calvin and Luther;[19] on sanctification, he approved the pre-Tridentine Romans. Only the Methodists, said he, had got the hang of holding the two together.[20]

That Wesley was a synergist can scarcely be denied unless "synergism" be defined in terms exclusively Pelagian. This, of course, was exactly what the Moravians and others tried to do to him, both before and after Aldersgate. But Wesley went on his way unruffled by this, and the Methodists, generally, have followed his emphasis on grace at work among the virtuous pagans and his implicit appeals for preaching to the unconverted in terms of that prevenient, preparatory grace that can be assumed active even in the unheeding heart.[21]

[18] *John Wesley*, pp. 3-33. See also, Albert C. Outler, "Theologische Akzente," in *Der Methodismus*, "Die Kirchen der Welt," VI, C. Ernst Sommer, ed. (Stuttgart: Evangelisches Verlagswerk, 1968), 84-102.

[19] *John Wesley*, p. 78. See also pp. 136-40.

[20] *Ibid.*, pp. 107-8.

[21] *Ibid.*, pp. 231-37.

In the blurred days before Aldersgate, it was Peter Böhler, probing the causes of Wesley's infirm faith, who identified and deplored this strand in Wesley's background: *Mi frater, mi frater, excoquenda est ista tua philosophia* ("My brother, my brother, that philosophy of yours must be purged away").[22] This was not, in the first instance at least, a blanket repudiation of *all* philosophy as such. Rather, as the context shows, it was a specific hit at what I would like to call the *"transactional* synergism" that Wesley had grown up with. Its main confidence was that if a man behaved according to his highest lights (*facere quod in se est*), his claim to saving grace had the status of a *right*. It was *this* "philosophia" (itself a misinterpretation of the *Homilies*) that had sterilized Wesley's dedication and zeal since his conversion in 1725. This is what had to go, and this is what did go at Aldersgate. What came in its place—but not all at once— is what we might call *"covenantal* synergism," in which both prevenient *and* saving grace are recognized as coordinate providential activities of the one true God of love who, in his love, makes and keeps covenant with faithful men. This doctrinal transformation continued to develop from his first encounter with Böhler until his first decisive results as a revival preacher in the spring of 1739.

Aldersgate, therefore, did not signify Wesley's abandonment of the *in se est* motif in his account of the drama of salvation. The proof of this is his vigorous repudiation of what he called "the German stillness," [23] his prompt counterattack against the Moravians, his withdrawal from the Fetter

---

[22] *Journal*, I, 440 (February 8, 1738): "I understood him not, and least of all when he said, *Mi frater*, etc."

[23] Cf. *John Wesley*, pp. 221,347, 353-54.

Lane Society, and his move to the Foundery. One might even say that the Methodist societies began a protest movement in favor of the *facere in se est*.[24]

The climax of this particular quarrel came in the famous debate with Zinzendorf (June 16, 1741) in Gray's Inn Walks in Holborn.[25] The point at issue, accepted as such by both men, was whether *any* of the works of grace are inherent, or if *all* are imputed. Said the Count, in a fine fury:

> I know of no such thing as inherent perfection [the final implication of *in se*] in this life. This is the error of errors. I pursue it everywhere with fire and sword! I stamp it under foot! I give it over to destruction! Christ is our only perfection. Whoever affirms inherent perfection denies Christ. . . .
>
> W. Isn't every true believer holy?
> Z. Indeed. But holy in Christ, not *in himself*. . . .
>
> W. It follows, then, that he is holy *in se*, doesn't it?
> Z. No. No! Only in Christ! Not holy *in se*. No one has any holiness *in se*.[26]

We well remember that Wesley's heart was strangely warmed while "one was reading Luther's preface to the *Epistle to the Romans*." [27] And it is well not to forget the deep affinities between Wesley and Luther as touching the heart

---

[24] Cf. *Journal*, II, 328-31; see also *John Wesley*, pp. 357 ff.

[25] Cf. *John Wesley*, pp. 367-72.

[26] It seems most unlikely that Zinzendorf had ever read Luther's September, 1517, *Disputation*—but here he is echoing even its language; see above, p. 56.

[27] *Journal*, I, 475 (May 24, 1738).

and marrow of the gospel of faith. But these two great men stood poles apart in the total configurations of their doctrines and their practical conceptions of evangelism, Christian nurture, and holiness—and the polarity was focused in this issue of the human *in se*.[28]

Again, in relation to Calvin and the English Puritans, it is true that Wesley was deeply indebted to the modified Calvinism of Amyraldus and his colleagues at Saumur. And yet the longest and most painful controversy of his life—zealously protracted by the American Methodists throughout the nineteenth century—was with the Calvinists about predestination. Here again, the *casus belli* was divine prevenience and human agency. *The Arminian Magazine* (which monopolized Wesley's literary output from 1777 until his death) was the cockpit of the conflict. The bite of the Calvinist critique, which has been all too successful in fixing the theological stereotypes by which Methodists have been subsequently judged and have all too often judged themselves, was that Wesley's profession of justification by faith was nullified by his overgenerous allowance for the human *in se*: that, in effect, he was either a poor theologian or else a Pelagian heretic. Wesley laid ream to ream in reasoned refutation of all this, but occasionally he was provoked to a dangerous candor: "Who was Pelagius?" asked one of his loyal but uncomprehending followers, prodded by Calvinist scorn. "By all I can pick up from ancient authors," Wesley retorts, "I guess he was both a wise and an holy man." [29] In a sermon written at the height of the controversy (April 28, 1784), he let fly with this annoyed outburst:

[28] *John Wesley*, p. 366.
[29] Letter to Alexander Coates, July 7, 1761. *Letters*, IV, 158.

I verily believe, the real heresy of Pelagius was neither more nor less than this: The holding that Christians may, by the grace of God, (not without it; that I take to be a mere slander,) "go on to perfection;" or, in other words, "fulfil the law of Christ."

"But St. Augustine says:"—When Augustine's passions were heated, his word is not worth a rush. And here is the secret: St. Augustine was angry at Pelagius: Hence he slandered and abused him, (as his manner was,) without either fear or shame.[30]

This is scarcely a balanced judgment, even for Wesley. But it reveals the intensity of his conviction that his own version of the paradox of sovereign grace and human freedom fell safely inside the orbit of orthodoxy and was not to be discredited by defamatory labels. One of the very best among the sermons of his old age is entitled "On Working Out Our Own Salvation" (1785).[31] Gabriel Biel could not have written it, but he would have understood it. Luther and Calvin would have rejected it out of hand.

In all of this, however, Wesley never faltered in his faithfulness to the Protestant premise of God's sovereignty and the gratuity of grace. On this score, he was as consistent as in his advocacy of the catholic tradition of human agency, and even more insistent. His constant stress on the *sola scriptura*, on justification by faith alone, on private judgment, and on the rights of nonconformity drew harsh criticism from the traditionalists in the Church of England, and this might have fitly ranked him with other Anglican evangelicals (Harris, Whitefield, Lady Huntingdon's chaplains, *et al.*)—except for their objections to his emphasis on divine-human inter-

[30] "The Wisdom of God's Counsels," *Works*, VI, 328-29.
[31] *Ibid.*, VI, 506-13.

action. In the other direction, Wesley had important affinities with the catholic traditions of the Nonjurors and High Churchmen in the area of prayer and devotion, but his Puritan brand of sacramental theology and church polity was plainly alien to them. He was a defender of reason in theology, and yet he stood at odds with Joseph Butler and even with a moderate like "John Smith," who roundly denounced his doctrine of "perceptible inspiration." [32] He understood himself as missionary and evangelist, an "extraordinary messenger" raised up in, and for the service of, the Church of England. During his lifetime, therefore, he compelled the British Methodists to seek and find their sacraments in the Established Church, although the course he set for them was almost bound to lead to eventual separation.

In America, the Methodists quickly organized themselves after the Revolution into the first "American" church— "Methodist Episcopal"—with a set bias against their Anglican background. The result was that the fact of our Anglican heritage has never been a vivid resource for our self-understanding as a denomination. Despite our repressed memories, however, Methodist preachers and theologians continued their development of the Wesleyan synthesis of God's gratuity and man's agency. By now, however, the term "Arminian" had lost its force as an epithet and had been adopted as a proud badge—supported by the revised history that the Methodist commitment to man's moral agency actually stemmed from Arminius and the Remonstrants. Our first systematic theologian, Richard Watson (1781-1833), begins

[32] Cf. the correspondence between Wesley and "John Smith" in Henry Moore's *Life of John Wesley*, (London, 1824-25), II, 277-322.

his *Theological Institutes* (1823) with a chapter on "Man as Moral Agent" and concludes it thus:

Those actions which among men have almost universally been judged *good*, have the implied sanction of the will of our wise and good Creator, being found in experience, and by the constitution of our nature and of human society, most conducive to happiness.[33]

This is later connected with prevenient grace: "His [man's moral] agency, even when rightly directed, is upheld and influenced by the superior power of God, and yet so as to be still his own." [34] This comes at the end of one of the longest sections in the book, which is—what else?—a refutation of Calvinism!

The core of Thomas Ralston's *Elements of Divinity*[35] is found in his three center chapters:

XVIII. *Calvinism and Arminianism Compared*
    ("The atonement so extends to *all* men as to render salvation possible for them," p. 238.)

XIX.   *The Moral Agency of Man*
    ("The whole history of the fall, in the light of reason, of common sense, and in view of all that we know of the Divine character and government, proclaims, in language clear and forcible, the doctrine of man's free moral agency," p. 249.)

XX.   *The Moral Agency of Man—Objections*
    ("So far from being absurd in itself, it [the doctrine

---

[33] (Nashville, Tennessee: Southern Methodist Publishing House, 1860), Part I, i, p. 10.

[34] *Ibid.*, Part II, xxviii, p. 610.

[35] (Louisville, Kentucky: Morton & Griswald, 1847).

of free agency] presents the only consistent illustration of the Divine attributes, and the only satisfactory comment upon the Divine administration," p. 257.)

William B. Pope, the most eminent of all nineteenth-century Methodist theologians, says nothing about the *quod in se est* maxim and yet teaches its import with triumphalist enthusiasm:

This hearer of the Word has a preliminary grace in the roots of his nature. . . . Redemption is universal and goes back to the root of [human] nature.[36]

[Methodism] has, however, more fully and consistently than the Remonstrant system, connected the universality of grace with the universality of redemption.[37]

There is, doubtless, to be sometimes found in men not yet regenerate, . . . in men not even decided in their choice, something of moral excellence.

On the whole, it may be said that the doctrine [of man's fallen nature] thus stated is the only one in harmony with all the facts in the case: it omits nothing, softens nothing, evades nothing.[38]

Miner Raymond, a key figure in Methodism's belated reception of the new European liberal theology, is still more explicit:

The universal consciousness of sin and of obligation to virtue proves that the race, as a rule, have, in actual, personal possession, all the elements essential to a moral character. . . . Whatever is

[36] Pope, *Compendium of Christian Theology* (New York: Phillips and Hunt, 1881), III, 366.
[37] *Ibid.*, p. 80.
[38] *Ibid.*, p. 82.

essential to moral obligation is not left to the contingencies of a man's circumstances. . . . Power, or ability to bring something to pass; intelligence, or ability to apprehend an end and its means; free-will, ability to do or not to do, and an apprehension of obligation, constitute the elements of a moral action, and all men are conscious of possessing these elements.[39]

Raymond marks the bare beginnings of the impact of German Protestant liberalism on American Methodism. Within two decades this influence had become a dominant one, with the result that the traditional Wesleyan synergism was swiftly transformed into a different type of theological anthropology. German liberalism was a metamorphosis of Lutheran and Reformed traditions and, as we have seen, not at all the same thing as the traditional Anglican version of the grace and nature paradox. Consequently, the experience of American Methodists turning "liberal," or whatever, has typically an odd and off-key character.

Let me say once more—because it *is* a ticklish point, easily misunderstood—that it is no part of my argument that synergism is the whole story about Methodist theology; it is not even its heart and spring. Of conscious and set purpose, Methodists have claimed as their own the main core of common Christian belief and then have produced a special mix of its catholic and evangelical elements. Out of this came Wesley's version of the doctrine of "salvation, faith and good works,"[40] the crown of which was his doctrine of perfection ("the fullness of faith," man's hope of becoming fully human). And it might be worth remarking that, in this view,

[39] Raymond, *Systematic Theology* (Cincinnati: Hitchcock and Walden, 1877), II, 314-15.
[40] *John Wesley*, pp. 123-33.

holiness is related to sanctifying grace much as the *facere in se est* is to prevenient grace.

What I do mean to urge, however, is that Wesley's accent on synergism affected the internal balance of his doctrinal perspective, that it generated its own distinctive hermeneutic for interpreting the Christian message as a whole, that its conscious practical concern is to serve the twin tasks of evangelism and Christian nurture, which have always been our main business in the world, even when we have not done them well.

There is, however, still another side to this problem of Methodist synergism and our role in the ecumenical dialogue. The Methodist theological complex has never been a stable entity by itself—and was never meant to be. In Wesley's own time, it was contained and sustained by the doctrinal and liturgical context of the Church of England, which provided the Methodist societies with a sacramental environment. Outside such an atmosphere Methodism has had perennial problems of theological identity that have encouraged an eclectic drift. This is obvious in the motley crowd of borrowed fashions in doctrine that we have sported from time to time: pietism, revivalism, fundamentalism, liberalism, neo-orthodoxy, existentialism, radical theology, neoclassical theism (you name it; we've got it around here somewhere!). For more than half a century now, it would seem that Methodist theologians have felt some sort of compulsion to "marry outside the clan." Concurrently, the fate of the scholarly study of Wesley and of Methodist constitutional history has sagged from bad to worse—so that, for example, the job of a badly needed critical edition of Wesley's *Works* (which the Oxford University Press has promised to publish and which would be of genuine ecumenical significance) is now languishing for want of adequate personnel. Or, again, supposing that such a strange impulse arose, where would one go for training as a Wesley specialist? This is not mere grumbling on my part. The consequences are serious—all the more so in a time when so much useful work is being done in the primary sources of the other Christian traditions, in an ecumenical style and on behalf of an ecumenical theology.

In any case, it is clear that the Methodist doctrinal perspective was not meant to stand on its own, apart from all the others. It works best in a wider and more catholic context where the humanist drag of the *in se* tradition is, or can be, redeemed in a sacramental order where grace and the means of grace are integrated in a visible and universal covenant: "unity, witness, and service" (to borrow a phrase from the New Delhi Assembly of the World Council of Churches). But by the same token, the Wesleyan heritage also profits from the constant criticism and correction of the evangelical emphasis on faith as a sheer gift, the evangelical horror of idolatry and ecclesiastical egoism. Thus, our constant need of challenge from the Lutherans, Calvinists, and Radical Protestants!

There may be those who find this description of the Methodist theological configuration unpromising or unimpressive. It does suggest a real deficiency, as if Methodist theology *needed* an ecumenical context in order to do well. And that, precisely, is my point, and I see at least two ways in which it is relevant to our future. In the first place, that future must surely lie with those who conceive theology in ecumenical terms above all else. The day of denominational theologies is over. The least productive of all theological approaches is the one that asks, "Which, among the rival options before us, is the one true system of doctrine?" Yet this has been our general habit in the Christian community for at least the past four polemical centuries. There is no call for Methodists to deprecate or jettison their heritage, nor offer to swap it off for something better. This witness that I have spoken of is still vital and relevant—never more so than today, and tomorrow—for its possible correction and balancing of traditions that lie to its right or left. We have a vital linkage with every major bloc in Christendom, and yet our independent mission in the modern world continues to cast us in a role that needs to be maximized within a catholic whole: as catalysts, critics, and pragmatists.

There is still another count on which our heritage can have prepared us for a hopeful future if we will claim and exploit it rightly. Is there a more obvious and massive problematic in modern theology than the escalating interest one sees everywhere in a credible doctrine of man (*in se*)—this vivid preoccupation with the human side of the God-man relationship, with man's place in nature and society, with man's responsibility for human culture, with the equivalence of salvation and human fulfilment? Pelagianism and synergism are no longer "dirty words" (secularism is the latest sacred cow!)— which accounts in large part for the swift eclipse of neo-orthodoxy within the last decade. And yet the old nemesis remains, and has already begun to strike back: man's preoccupation with man is the threshold of his declension into humanism; glib talk of human fulfillment (what Wesley called, in a different context, "holiness of heart and life") may readily lead to the disparagement or denial of grace. "The death of God" is a natural event in any situation where the God-man relationship is construed in terms of disjunctive *rivalry!*

There is, therefore, a vital mission in the modern world for a theology in search of catholicity, a theology that struggles for the balancing of the God-man paradox, a theology that holds the middle between fideism and moralism, between "evangelical" and "catholic," between the pneumatic and sacramental dimensions of the church. This cannot mean an antiquarian return to Wesley or to anybody else as arbitrary authority. Wesley was the first to repudiate *that* sort of thing. Even so, there is still something about his way of doing theology that is still open to us as paradigm: (1) to ground it all in Scripture; (2) to match it all against the centuries and the Christian consensus; (3) to keep chording the keys of grace *and* agency together; (4) to remember, always, the aim of it all: effective mission in the world, effective service to the world for which Christ died. For us and for our future, is there a conceivable alternative more promising?

iii
the methodist world movement: a servant of the ecumenical

Some months ago I was a member of a committee created by the World Methodist Council to investigate the feasibility of founding an office for world Methodism at the World Council of Churches building in Geneva. We traveled to the Swiss city and put our question both to Dr. Eugene Carson Blake, General Secretary of the World Council, and to Dr. W. A. Visser 't Hooft, his predecessor. In the course of our talks Mr. Charles Parlin, the Methodist chairman, raised this question with the two noted ecumenists: "Do you think that in a day of ecumenical advance Methodism is justified in setting up a denominational office? Would it not be interpreted as an anti-ecumenical act?" Dr. Visser 't Hooft replied, Dr. Blake concurring: "There was a time when I would have viewed the establishment of an international denominational office as a roadblock on the way to a truly universal church. But I am a realist. I am convinced now that for the foreseeable future the real strength of Christianity will continue to be in its confessions. By all means, bring your office to Geneva." He went on to add, "If Methodism were to be destroyed tonight, it would reappear tomorrow, perhaps under another name if not its own. World confessionalism is a settled feature of ecumenical existence in our time."

Perhaps the distinguished ecumenical leader has given a clue to the direction ecumenism will take in the days ahead. Possibly the hour of synthesis is at hand in the ecumenical movement. The first world Christianity was largely an extension of denominational Christianity—the Alliance of Reformed Churches, the Baptist World Alliance, the Lutheran World Federation, the Lambeth Conference of Anglican Bishops, the World Convention of the Churches of Christ, not to mention the World Methodist Council. The burgeoning ecumenical movement, quite naturally, saw these confessional bodies as a threat to its own forward progress. The conventional ecumenist of the first days had no palate for world denominationalism. He saw confessionalism as costly, superfluous, reactionary, perpetuating organizational and institutional rituals that by every rule ought to disappear. He offered ecumenism as a fresh, vigorous antithesis to world confessionalism. Perhaps the hour has come when the ecclesiastical statesman will draw a new synthesis. Without denying the ecumenical vision for a moment he will see in world confessionalism a stage on the way, representing truth and strength which will at last incorporate themselves in the great church.

Here are vast potential resources for the ecumenical movement. The world confessions are expressions of going religious organizations at home. To work for their undoing makes about as much sense to the average church member as the abolition of the United States in favor of an ideal world state yet to be. The Methodist church through its far-flung missionary program is found in almost every section of the world, exerting tremendous influence on the solution of the world's economic and social problems. Confessionalism is a training ground for ecumenical leadership: how many of the great ecumenical leaders got their start in denominational churches! Through the vast denominational enterprises they have been thrown into acquaintanceship with comparable leaders of other branches of the church. Furthermore, these denominational bodies have a loyalty attaching to them far more extensive than any present ecumenical organization. Their benevolences reach astronomical figures. To represent them, of course, as the only spiritual realities of our time is to dwell in the pre-ecumenical age. But to think that confessional disagreements have been overcome and that a radically new ecumenical age is about to dawn, or that denominations have no longer any contribution to make to the fullness of the church, is premature and unrealistic. Truly prophetic leadership in our time will bring these world movements with their tribute, material and spiritual, into the treasury of ecumenism.

I am asking specifically, therefore, What does world Methodism have to contribute to the ecumenical movement?

The first service is a negative one. World Methodism can help prevent identifying the ecumenical movement with national churches. The last General Conference of The United Methodist Church gave autonomy to thirteen of its overseas conferences, in order that they might affiliate, in most cases, with churches in their own lands. The Consultation on Church Union in the United States is essentially aiming at the establishment of a national church. These endeavors are ecumenical in the sense that they contemplate a union of denominations. But the weaving together of disparate fellowships into a world community does not have top priority. Generally speaking, ecumenism with them halts at the waterline. A case could be made in some instances for the proposition that they are nationalism clad in ecclesiastical vesture.

A national church is as defective ecumenically as a denominational one. Both are compromises with the universalism inplied by the gospel. Yes, national churches contain many—perhaps all—of the gospel's strains within their membership. But so do denominational churches. We scarcely ever open an urban Methodist church without there being fully as many non-Methodists as Methodists within the charter membership. National churches are often ecumenically oriented in the broadest sense. The same is true of some denominations. But both the church that limits its membership to those who affirm a stated creed or share a heritage and the one that draws its boundaries to coincide with the nation are only approximations of ecumenism. The church in ideal is as far above differences of race and political allegiance as it is above denominational pride. The Christian impulse no more respects national sovereignty than a radio impulse requires a visa to enter a country. A "national" church is a round square, a wooden iron—a contradiction. Strangely, many of our ecumenical enthusiasts have not seen this elemental fact that nationalism, ecclesiastical as well as political, is essentially an affront to the universalism of the gospel. The presence of a worldwide church like the Methodist is, if nothing more, a reminder of the more than national character of the Christian fellowship.

The so-called national church is not only wanting in principle; it is also a practical threat. For it has the resources of a national community behind it. It has the might of popular sentiment going for it, and international experience in the last decades would testify that there is nothing stronger in the modern world. Even international communism has been forced to bow to it. The nation for modern man has a sanctity that justifies its being called "modern man's other religion." For a generation Reinhold Niebuhr has inveighed against the idolatrous character of our state worship. How self-righteous the state is! How resentful of the judgments of religion! The state is guilty of monstrous egotism. It claims universality for parochial values, seeing its own pattern of life as a norm for others, and, when it does not receive the adulation it expects, interprets the rejection as a threat to its security. It claims a pseudo-immortality. Hitler was not the first nor last to contend that he was building a Reich that would last a thousand years. Behind this rejection of essential Christianity, nationalism puts the strongest concentrations of power ever known to man. And its appetite for more and more power increases with its satisfaction. It is no wonder that the state has often been the church's persecutor—aggressive and brutal, often threatening the survival of the Christian community.

How can a national church survive *as a church?* How can it hope to exercise prophetic criticism? How can it be "the people of God" when it draws its sustenance and takes its orders from Mammon? How can it develop its own life, when it is subject to the state? How can a national church reverse the downward trend toward becoming more national than Christian? Perhaps in long-settled democracies like those of the Anglo-Saxon world, a church can be national without being at the same time a color-bearer for the state. But the lands where national churches are emerging are often wanting in stable democratic traditions. National churches in these countries will be forced, when a crisis calls for a show of strength, into ways unecumenical.

John R. Mott once remarked that he would rather belong to the worst hardscrabble denomination that was global in its thrust and interest than to the best national church he had ever seen. He follows in the steps of his spiritual father, John Wesley. In the *Minutes* of the Methodist Conference for 1747 the following question and answer appear, the answer presumably by Wesley:

> Question: "What instance or ground is there then in the New Testament for a *National* Church?"
> Answer: "We know none at all. We apprehend it to be a merely political institution."

Supranational churches are not without resources, too, for the furtherance of cosmic Christianity. An international church, like the international Red Cross, can gain entrée to places of service when the doors are barred to nationals. Bishop Frederick Wunderlich, recently retired, has told me that when he sought admission to East Germany to conduct his conferences, he often met resistance from the authorities of East Germany. They called him a West German, trying to get through the Wall for no good purpose. But he always had a trump! He could prove that he was a bishop of a world church. That never failed to breach the Wall and open opportunities for service.

What form must The United Methodist Church assume if it is to remedy the situation created by autonomous Methodist churches? The standing Committee on the Structure of Methodism Overseas (COSMOS) is at work on the problem, as is also the World Methodist Council. It is plain that a General Conference meeting in the United States of America to legislate for churches in South America and Malaysia is not the answer. There is a vast bulk of General Conference legislation that churches overseas find irrelevant to their life.

They need simple, elastic structures that a *Discipline* written in the United States does not satisfy, despite the good intentions of those who frame it.

Two proposals being studied by COSMOS seem viable. The first is a Methodist World Church with a truly international General Conference. Its unity would consist in a common basis of faith, ministry, membership, and general episcopacy. The General Conference would legislate only on matters of international concern. In addition to the highest conference there would be regional conferences—one for the United States, one for Europe, one for Africa, one for Asia, one for Latin America. The regional conferences would have authority to write their own *Disciplines*, providing administration and organization suited to the region. This plan would utilize the present form of church structure, but reduce the American General Conference to the status of a central conference, parallel to the conferences in other continents. Supremacy would belong to a truly World General Conference.

The second plan would create a conference of Methodist churches, consisting of regional churches meeting at a world level for consultative purposes. The Green Lake Missionary Consultation of October, 1966, is a possible prototype. Such a polity would be looser in discipline than the first plan, perhaps less "connectional" but possibly more congenial to the surging nationalism of the newer churches, who desire to throw off parental restraint without losing the family heritage and friendly ties. Somehow we must frame a new structure that will deliver us from the specter of "nationalistic" Christianity, bequeathing freedom to the younger Christian communities to make their own decisions yet integrating them with a treasured family solidity.

"Before I die," said Donald Soper, the distinguished former president of the British Methodist Conference, "I hope to see the Church *in* England taking the place of the Church *of* England." It seems to me that such a worthy end is more likely to be achieved if Methodism does not lose its world character during the years of transition.

As a second service, Methodism as a world movement can offer specific suggestions for bringing ecumenical unity into fruitful relationship with its correlate, diversity. So often in the ecumenical movement we have united men by neglecting their differences. What we need, as William Temple once wrote, is a unity "frankly based on difference, where men desire to learn from one another while holding fast to all that they have found true or precious." [1] A connectional church with branches in many places can offer experience in the blending of unity with difference. Unity *per se* is self-defeating, whether in the church or in society at large. Unity in itself tends to rigidity, sluggishness. United churches are seldom exemplars of vitality. There is no magic in unity whereby the mere contact of dead bodies generates life. It ought not to be, perhaps, but churches holding a monopoly rarely put forth maximum effort.

The larger the church, too, the less it offers in intimate fellowship. Further, there is little to become excited about in the meager uniformity of the common denominator. The specious ecumenicity which fears to offend and endeavors to accommodate everything to everything will never draw

[1] *Essays in Christian Politics and Citizenship and Kindred Subjects* (London, New York: Longmans, Green, and Co, 1927), p. 7.

blood from the martyrs. Generally speaking, the larger the group the lower the average; what is done in the name of unity will not escape that law. If the union of churches is to justify itself eventually, it must also make the church more moral. Experience shows, however, that the moralization of the church comes from the small group, the movements, some of which border on separation. From another angle, an organization may become so large that it devours its makers. It becomes a foe of freedom. It becomes unwieldy. Its very dimensions prevent effective oversight. What Justice Louis Brandeis said about the limitation of human capacity to rule a corporation applies with equal force to the management of a church: "There are many men who are all wool, but none are more than a yard wide!"

Methodism has a heritage which may be useful in bringing unity and diversity into fruitful interaction. Wesley thought of his movement as an evangelical, or at least personal-religion, variant within the general church. He contended to his death that he had not actually separated from the Church of England. He not only stayed within that church himself, but he endeavored to keep the Methodists within the fold, even to the point of setting Methodist services at an hour which would not compete with the services of the Established Church. Wesley saw value in the unity of the church which could not be found in any form of sect.

Yet he saw the shortcomings of the Church of England, too, especially its want of life. He devised his societies, therefore, "to beget, preserve, and increase" the divine life in the church. He never thought of them as churchly in the usual sense: their function was particular, not universal; they were agencies for the cleansing of the church and nation by spreading "scriptural holiness." They proclaimed no new doctrine, unless we may call holiness "new" by virtue of the infrequency of its appearance. The societies had no ecclesiastical authority: men could take or leave them as they pleased. They were designed, furthermore, as temporary expedients; Wesley once remarked that in the beginning he did not expect the Methodist movement to last above thirty years. They were a particular palliative for an immediate situation, not intended, like the church, to be from everlasting to everlasting. *Methodism is an emphasis that became an institution.* It has useful experience to offer concerning both the unity required by an institution and the diversity exemplified by an emphasis.

Smaller unofficial unities serve the larger. Has there ever been an enduring renewal of religion without the spontaneous activity of small groups for mutual encouragement, fellowship, and common effort? The cell group is one of the marks of Christian genius. In any considerable aspiration toward catholicity there must be room for groups of like-minded members who give themselves to the development of particular phases of truth and practice. They make their largest contribution to the whole by developing and maintaining their specialty. In promotion, money can be raised for general causes through particular agencies. How often, as we have said, the ecumenical leadership of our time has come from communities not aspiring to be ecumenical! What the church owes to the older Student Christian Movement, less than ecumenical in its totality, individualistic in its piety; yet, such as it had it gave unbegrudgingly to world Christianity.

Our task in the ecumenical movement is to develop organic pluralism. The church that is to be must have a plan for the many. The many sentiments that cluster about Christianity must have appropriate means of expression. There must be a place in the church for the individual, since he, not the organization, is the ultimate (human) subject. As Harold Roberts reminded the 1966 World Methodist Conference, "There is no such thing as an ecumenical baby." Every baby is born of particular parents, in a particular community, with a body and mind like no other. The church must ever be aware of this elementary fact.

Yet the many must be organically related to each other. There must be direction and a constitution binding on all. The many must be in fruitful interrelation. Differences will persist, but they must not be allowed to destroy; rather they must supplement and enrich one another. The church must sing the gospel song not in unison but in harmony. Each may have its own pitch and quality, yet at the same time reinforce and enrich the others. Part of the reason for the fragmentizing of Christianity lies not in the perversity of human nature, but in the intrinsic character of the gospel. It is not "simple," as we sometimes say. While it begins with the familiar facts and experiences of everyday, the deeper our acquaintance with it the more we discover its capacity for endless application and the multifarious aspects it presents to different minds.

Some of us recall a notable sermon preached years ago by the late Halford Luccock of Yale, in which he used an illustration clipped from a small Vermont town newspaper. It stated, "Last Thursday evening at the P.T.A., Mabel Jones whistled the Fifth Symphony." Professor Luccock's comment was that while Mabel was probably a nice girl and quite likely an accomplished performer, she could not possibly have whistled Beethoven's Fifth! It takes a symphony to do that, a symphony of many instruments under a harmonious central direction. The gospel, too, requires for its rendition a community that is both many and one.

What does this mean practically? The blueprint for the great church is yet to be drawn. Ecumenists assure us that the one church will provide opportunities for differences of religious interest and expression. But so much effort has, naturally, been expended in the promotion of unity that little attention has been given to how a saving diversity can be assured. The Roman Catholic Church has given instance of how this may be done by its oneness of creed, ministry, sacraments, and constitutional direction with its diversities of ministration, represented by orders. For want of a better solution we might take it as a provisional pattern. One of the leading Methodist ecumenists in Britain has suggested, for instance, that the Methodists might prepare themselves to become a preaching order in the universal church. Professor Outler has likened Wesley to a "superior-general" of an evangelical order within a regional division of the church catholic.[2] Certainly this type of structure is not entirely alien to our experience. The great Protestant church families are steadily congealing into a few types. Perhaps they may become orders in the one church, at least to begin with. Time must dictate the form that the diversities will take, but it is not too early for us, especially Methodists, to lend our thought and experience to the means of securing both unity and difference in the ultimate church.[3]

[2] *John Wesley*, Albert C. Outler, ed., p. 306.
[3] Hans Küng strongly argues the case for continuing diversity (though not disunity) among the churches in *The Church* (New York: Sheed and Ward, 1968). He maintains that "the unity of the Church, moreover, not only

Suppose as a practical goal American ecumenists would concentrate on two items. First, we would endeavor to unify our several ministries. Such an achievement would carry with it intercommunion, intercelebration, and the exchange of members. While the prospect of such an achievement is not an easy one, it would meet most of the reproaches against our divided condition. It is the fact that despite our professions of fellowship we are still not willing to acknowledge equality of status to our several ministries that is the serpent in our ecumenical garden!

Secondly, suppose that we formulated a viable—and mandatory—scheme of comity for our cities. We often wail about the overchurched character of our towns and cities. But we do not have more churches than our population can sustain. Our parishes, however, are often poorly placed and proportioned, particularly in the cities. Suppose that we were to unite our ministries constitutionally and provide an overall plan of proceeding in our growing urban culture. I believe that we could leave nature to take its course concerning our diversities. Our present denominations under an umbrella of theological and practical unity would slowly shrink into something approximating orders, and the church would be one though many.

The ecumenical movement needs leadership with bifocal vision. The cloud by day and fire by night, drawing us to a final unity, must still go before us. But we must also be able to see the near-at-hand and take responsibility for finding

presupposes a multiplicity of Churches, but makes it flourish anew: through the diversity of God's callings, through the multiplicity of the gifts of the Spirit given to the Church, through the variety of the members of Christ and their functions" (p. 274).

divergent expressions of the Christian impulse to match the God-given differences implicit in the gospel and our multitudinous human nature. As we have said, worldwide Methodism may be in every land a servant of *unam multiplex*. Our slogan for many years has been the word of Wesley, "The Methodists are one people." A multiplicity of individuals united in one inheritance and fellowship! We can minister through our experience to making the citizens of the world one *Christian* people.

Once more, our worldwide denominationalism may be a theological influence for what its father, John Wesley, referred to as "experimental religion." It is what we would call today "experiential" or practical religion. It means validation of both faith and ecclesiastical form by experienced facts, by what a person may verify in his own experience. It accepts the worth of prayer, for instance, not because the Bible celebrates it, but because men actually find value when they pray. Christ is the Savior, not because New Testament prophecy proclaims it and the Creed affirms it, but because contemporary experience confirms it. "Experimental religion" means that whatever makes no practical difference does not matter; that which is alleged to be good is not good, unless it is experienced as good.

"Experimental religion" is the doctrine, first of all, that God's love can be experienced firsthand. He witnesses by his Spirit to our spirits that he is our Father. We may be blessed with his presence. He may be the companion of our way. We may have inner assurance that we are in favor with him. Faith is not just a wishful hope; it can be a triumphant certainty. God speaks immediately to the heart, granting abounding peace and joy and zeal.

> If e'er when faith had fall'n asleep,
> I heard a voice, "Believe no more,"
> And heard an ever-breaking shore
> That tumbled in the Godless deep,
>
> A warmth within the breast would melt
> The freezing reason's colder part,
> And like a man in wrath the heart
> Stood up and answer'd, "I have felt."
> (Tennyson, *In Memoriam*)

Our experiences of God's love and our loving response to it can grow from more to more. Justification by faith in God's forgiving love is the beginning. Faith achieves its fullness in the regeneration of all life. Holiness, the experienced domination of the whole life by love, becomes the trademark of the mature Christian.

To be sure, holiness of life has not been appreciated by all ecumenists: it has sometimes been associated with pentecostalism and pietism, which are not pre-eminently ecclesiastical in their orientation. Yet the insistence on experienced spiritual excellence is a force making for universality. Insist that a person must belong to a certain nation or subscribe to a certain creed, and there is an inevitable narrowing. But make holiness the mark of the church, by virtue of God's grace vouchsafed to all men, and the walls of racial and intellectual separation go down. "Whosoever will" may come in.

"Experimental religion" is not only experienced inwardly as faith; it is expressed outwardly as love. God works in us to produce good works outside us. To use the evangelical idiom, we not only know we are saved, but others know we are saved. As Dr. Johnson put it vividly, "When a man becomes a Christian, even his dog and his cat can tell it." Faith works by love. Faith in Christ's pardoning mercy makes one loving, and love causes one to do what is right for the brother. Genuine, experienced faith comes to fruit in good behavior. For our time the love induced by faith frequently goes into social service. Historically, and quite as validly, it has expressed itself in evangelism, the effort to lead others into the higher life. At the Evanston Assembly of the World Council of Churches in 1954, Dr. John R. Mott, then nearly ninety, was a visitor. When they asked him if he cared to say a word, the message of the veteran ecumenist, perhaps his last public utterance, consisted of one sentence: "When John R. Mott is dead remember him as an evangelist." Old-fashioned as such sentiment sounds, it expresses not only his denominational tradition, but suggests one of the great services an experimental religion could offer to ecumenism. For a good share of the churches in the ecumenical movement are not moving. Their membership is at a standstill or dwindling; their church schools are getting smaller; their missions have become little more than social service; while their finances are in arrears of rising costs.

An experimental religion places high value on the use of appropriate methods. Wesley was a pragmatist, even though whatever he found to "work" he also discovered in the Scripture. Bishop McConnell used to say of Wesley that while he was not a Jesuit, he judged every means by the results it got. For him the church was an instrument. The Lord's Supper was a "converting" ordinance. The episcopacy was not a theological doctrine; the bishop was an overseer who was to be judged by the fruit of his administration. (Paradoxically, had it not been for the "masterly inaction" of the Anglican bishops, Methodism would probably have been strangled in infancy. Un-Methodistic inactivity gave the Methodist movement its chance.) The minister was to be judged—as Wesley told the Bishop of London in a famous letter—by whether as a result of his preaching of the gospel

the habitual drunkard that was is now temperate in all things; the whoremonger now flees fornication; he that stole, steals no more, but works with his hands; he that cursed or swore, perhaps at every sentence, has now learned to serve the Lord with fear and rejoice unto Him with reverence; those formerly enslaved to various habits of sin are now brought to uniform habits of holiness.[4]

The demand for results is always stimulating, and it is needed in the ecumenical movement. For as a world phenomenon, it has been weighted heavily on the side of Reformation theology. There was a loose connection in Luther's thought between faith and works. It is generally distrustful of human effort. If faith is all sufficient, it is easy to reduce the means of grace to secondary importance. And not a few theologians of the Continental persuasion have made merry with the illusions of perfectionism and intoned against the awesome sinfulness of pride.

But if the ecumenical movement is truly ecumenical, i.e. universal, we must acknowledge that there is a biblical emphasis on holiness of life, without which we are told that no man shall see God. Granted, there is little merit in the mechanical and outward performance of church rites. But when we

---

[4] *Letters*, II, 290.

come to the issue from the biblical point of view, the good deeds flowing from a loving heart are not to be feared. Indeed, the more of them the better! Church unity is not an absolute, either in the New Testament or in the history of the church. Both as Protestants and as Methodists our forebears broke with the dominant ecclesiastical unities of their time because they found them spiritually wanting. A tradition like the Methodist has a place in the economy of God to raise the question as to the practical—the moral, if you will—worth of what we do. If Wesley were to confront the contemporary ecumenical issues, I do not imagine he would be greatly concerned about the doctrines of apostolic succession, or the nature of the sacraments, or the status of the diaconate. He was not when he was living. Some of them he pronounced "fables." He would more likely inquire about the reasons for our arrested growth in membership, our decline in young men presenting themselves for the ministry, our paltry stewardship, the absence of classes in experimental living, the coldness of our worship. He would probably say—and rightly—that unless the ecumenical movement can cure the unhealth of which these phenomena are symptoms, it does not matter much whether we are a part of it or not.

In the Book of Revelation there is a mighty vision of the holy city. The writer represents it as having twelve gates, "to the north three gates, to the south three gates, to the east three gates, to the west three gates" (21:13). If one were to treat the vision imaginatively and in connection with the ecumenical theme, he might portray it as a symbol of the geographical universality of the church. Men from every corner of the globe have rightful access to it. But the image is qualitatively suggestive, too. "To the north three gates"—

Athens is north of Jerusalem. The kingdom invites the intellectual to come. "To the east three gates"—the East, the Orient, the land of mysticism. Men may come by that way. "To the south three gates"—the land of warmth, of color, of romance. Those from the South have their place. Finally, "to the west three gates"—the throbbing, driving, practical, activistic West. Men from there also have a place in the church. The Methodists come by that fourth way. It is their responsibility in the ecumenical movement to keep it open and to bring their treasures therein.

iv
methodism: a world movement

John Wesley and George Whitefield used practically the same sentence in defending their right to preach different brands of Methodism outside the bounds prescribed by Anglican canon law: "I look upon all the world as my parish." [1] We may dismiss the problem of who was quoting whom (neither man gives the other credit for the sentence). One could say also that the kind of world consciousness which the expression suggests is that of a sniper-like, almost sectarian world-claiming which does not fare too well in the conclave of well-behaved ecclesiastical families. It is more important to note, however, that for them the world was not primarily the place for global organizations; it was the place for mission, the stage upon which the church carries out the command to announce the gospel and to call men to conversion. Methodism today dare not forget that this is the cradle of any world consciousness it may have achieved.

Although Wesley rejected this feature of canon law, we must remember that he did not reject the Church of England. He knew, however, that the revival would precipitate a response there. After disclaiming any intention to separate from the Anglican Church, he commented: "We believe notwithstanding, either that they [the Methodists] will be thrust out, or that they will leaven the whole Church." [2] To a certain extent both things happened. The Methodist awakening did leaven, in different ways and to different degrees, almost all the existing churches in Great Britain and even

[1] *Letters*, I, 286 (March 20, 1739); cf. *Journal*, II, 218 (June 11, 1739); Luke Tyerman, *The Life of the Rev. George Whitefield* (London: Hodder & Stoughton, 1890), I, 316.
[2] *Works*, VIII, 281 (June 26, 1744).

outside; the Methodist churches of today are only a few of the loaves resulting from the process. But some were also "thrust out." Our question today is whether the time has not arrived for the process to be reversed. Will not the mission of Methodism be best carried out by reintegrating the leaven within the lump?

I

To deal with this issue, we must first try to fix our bearings with reference to the theological problem, the ecclesiastical situation, and the secular setting involved in our subject.

1. Theologically, we are confronted with the question of catholicity, i.e., that quality of Christ's activity in the church which drives her toward all and toward the whole. Catholicity must not be understood statically or passively as the preservation of a given "totality" of doctrine, ministry, or mandate. It refers, on the one hand, to the pluridimensional movement of the Spirit *from* the One in whom all were called to newness *to* the all for whom he was sent. This movement takes place in the arena of human history and consequently finds expression in the always varied and concrete conditions of historical existence. Catholicity refers, on the other hand, to the church's search for integrity and full development of life—in each local situation in which it is placed as well as throughout the whole inhabited earth. Local "incarnation" and universal concern, communion and integration, must strive toward visibility. The church which is truly catholic endeavors to have its theological thought, liturgical response, structural design, and missionary thrust reflect the newness that the Spirit creates and discloses in each new historical

situation. It also endeavors to bear the identifiable imprints of the one Christ upon the doctrinal, ministerial, communal, missionary, and liturgical traditions of the people of God throughout history. The catholic church is marked by a readiness to follow Christ in his ministry of peace and justice into all the rifts and antagonisms of mankind, risking the pressures and tensions which this ministry awakens in the life of the church. It is marked too by the pastoral tenderness that watches over the fellowship of all the members.[3]

These somewhat abstract descriptions are intended to give theological focus to problems which concretely concern the consideration of Methodism as a world movement. They are meant to emphasize that "world movement" must be understood in relation to the tension between local integrity and universal connectionalism, contemporary adaptation and historical continuity, missionary impulse and internal unity.

2. The very term "Methodism" reminds us of the fact that the history of Christianity has run, at least for the last four centuries, on the rails of confessionalism. The self-understanding of these *confessions* or *confessional families* constitutes a very complex problem. On the one hand, it varies not only from one to the other, but also in the course of the history of each one of them. On the other hand, our present predicament is particularly perplexing: theologically our independent confessional existence is justified only by the claim that our particular confession embodies in a unique way the correct understanding of the gospel and the fullness of the church. But in actual practice, most churches (in-

---

[3] An attempt to emphasize this dynamic aspect of catholicity was made at the WCC Assembly at Uppsala, as is apparent in the preparatory document and the (somewhat toned down) Report of Section I. Cf. *Uppsala Report*, pp. 11-18.

cluding the Roman Catholic Church at certain points) are increasingly reluctant to make such a claim for themselves.

In this situation the confessions seem to be driven to a theory of complementarity which is highly questionable, both theologically and pragmatically. According to such a view, each of the existing confessions is "part" or "a branch" of the church universal, which is to be found—and consequently reconstructed—in the sum total of the "denominations" or "confessional families." This view is hardly justifiable in terms of the New Testament usage of the word "church" (for which the "churches" are not parts or sections but full embodiments and representations of "the church"). It is theologically unacceptable because it removes the "unity" and "catholicity" of the church—indeed its visible existence as such—to the realm of abstraction (a conceptual addition of existing churches) or futurity (the expected union). It minimizes the real differences among the denominations and consequently risks the indifferentism which Pope Pius XI saw and condemned. Finally it transforms "church union" into a jigsaw puzzle operation devoid of all urgency and dynamism.

Given such a situation, it is not surprising that more and more people feel that "the confessional age has come to an end." [4] The continuing existence of confessional structures at a time when, to say the least, we are very dubious about their justification creates an uneasiness and bad conscience which express themselves at times in aggressiveness and self-assertion and at other times in a clumsy ineffectiveness and

[4] The expression was used by the German Lutheran theologian Wolfgang Trillhaus in a Latin American Lutheran Congress in Lima (1965). Cf. *Ekklesia*, X (1966), 22-23.

hesitation. The problem is peculiarly acute for Methodism, which has never been conscious of a well-defined confessional identity (in doctrinal terms) and has almost openly subscribed to the idea of complementarity.[5]

Our Protestant confessional history reveals a further ambiguity. World confessional families have, on the one hand, provided a means for whatever measure of catholicity the churches have been able to realize in terms of historical and geographical continuity and connectionalism. They have been the instruments for the transmission of doctrinal, ministerial, and liturgical tradition. They have provided a universal family which has stretched the horizon of local groups and offered them a wider fellowship. They have obeyed a missionary vocation which has extended the family of God to the farthest corners of the earth. They have bridged separations of culture, caste, and race. On the other hand, honesty forces us to acknowledge that the "universality" of confessional families is shot through with artificiality, cultural alienation, sectarianism, domination, and rigidity which have hindered the manifestation of "local catholicity" and forced churches into a separate, narrow, and maimed existence.[6]

---

[5] The historical introduction to the 1964 *Discipline* of The Methodist Church, for instance, speaks (p. 10) of that church as "*a part* of the one Church of our Lord" (italics mine).

[6] When Argentine Lutherans are divided into "Missouri" and "United" Lutherans, and Brazilian Methodists into "Independent" and "Episcopal" Methodists; when the Methodist *Discipline* forces (for the sake of "connectionalism") into Latin America an institutional structure (the series of "conferences") which is totally foreign to our cultural tradition; when a denominational agency in the United States conceives and writes the literature which (translated into different languages) is supposed to root and nurture in the faith children in Kenya, Ceylon, Germany, and Venezuela—when all this happens, it is quite evident that we cannot speak of universality but only of universal domination by *one* local (American, European) national, cultural, linguistic pattern.

3. It is hardly necessary to state that the catholicity of the church finds expression always in the conditions of particular configurations of social, political, economic, and cultural factors. But it may not be useless to remind ourselves how such conditions affected both the origin and the expansion of Methodism. The imprint of the Industrial Revolution can be seen upon the values, norms, and ethos of early Methodism, especially as these were crystallized in the General Rules. Likewise, Methodism's expansion, occurring in the wake of British and American colonial and economic expansion, has naturally been shaped by the geographical patterns as well as influenced by the cluster of ideas, dependencies, and models developed in these historical processes.

We may summarize what has been said thus far by asserting that "world Methodism" is a particular realization of Christian catholicity shaped by the confessional pattern of Protestantism, by the Evangelical Awakening, and by nineteenth-century missionary expansion, the latter two ecclesiastical realities themselves significantly shaped by the Industrial Revolution and the colonial, ideological, and economic expansion of Great Britain and the United States of America.

II

We must now move from the background of the historical matrix which has shaped Methodism to the foreground of our present situation.

1. Our problem is that of a confessional movement in an ecumenical age. The ecumenicity of our time is established not only by the regular channels of the ecumenical movement, such as the World Council of Churches and regional, na-

tional, and city councils; it is also established by the fact that trends in theology, piety, and ethical stance move independently of confessional platforms. Less abstractly put: People cluster across and clash within denominational boundaries. Theological education cannot be conceived except in terms of multiconfessional faculties and student bodies—even in confessional institutions. The challenge of "secular ecumenism" explodes within and faces equally all confessional families. All this does not mean that we are moving into a time of increasing consensus and unification, but rather that the lines of division and tension which deploy the diversity and manifoldness of Christian understanding and life (and manifest the mystery of sin in the church as well) are totally unrelated to confessional boundaries. Our problem is how to relate the manifoldness of the Christian faith, hitherto shaped into confessional families by the cultural patterns of north European and American history, to the new diversity and the new patterns called forth by universal history in the latter part of the twentieth century (and how to counteract, as far as possible, the schism-creating power of evil). And this will mean not simply a reorganizing of old emphases and interpretations in new configurations, but the emergence and combination of genuinely new ones which the Holy Spirit creates and awakens in totally new situations.

2. To speak of the universal history of the latter part of the twentieth century is to speak of an increasingly unified *and* an increasingly divided world. The facts of the situation have been rehearsed so many times that I scarcely need to recall them. Modern technology has so interrelated all areas of the world that practically all human activities have a global reference. But that same technology, building upon an im-

balance in political, economic, and military power between the developed nations and the so-called "Third World," widens the already existing gap and condemns two thirds of the population and countries of the world to a growing dependence, social deterioration, and frustration. This situation poses extremely grave problems to all "world structures," whether political, economic, or ecclesiastical. Isolationism is impossible. Traditional ecclesiastical structures of world unity, however, built on the basis of a center in Western Europe or the United States (New York, London, Geneva, Rome, or any other place), reproducing the pattern of commercial or political colonialism, are unacceptable because they succeed only in perpetuating and even "sacralizing" the very kind of domination and alienation which countries in the Third World are determined to overcome. Our problem, therefore, is how to create conditions for real partnership, for the kinds of relations which promote and make possible local integrity as well as universal catholicity within the conditions of the contemporary world.

One must plumb the depths of the problem before talking too hastily about the task of world churches being to bridge the gaps in our world—as if that possibility were a mere consequence of their alleged "supranational" character. If a church in Rhodesia or in Guatemala, for instance, is called, in the name of catholic unity with Christians in Great Britain or in the United States, to divorce inself from the struggle against the segregationist or imperialist slavery imposed upon the people in its country by or with the aid of British and American power; if it is called to refrain from sharing in the tension and pathos which alone sustain those involved in this struggle; if it is suggested that participation in such movements amounts to ingratitude or even heresy—then the "unity" invoked is nothing more than a form of alienation. People in these "younger" churches may boast of their "overcoming" the narrow nationalism of their countrymen; Christians in the "powerful" countries may feel enthusiastic about the fellowship they enjoy "above" the tensions—and all the time each group may be deceiving itself and the other, and the demons of superiority, complacency, resentment, and bitterness may be preparing their harvest of destruction under the cover of a false peace. True reconciliation is not reached by avoiding the tensions and conflicts which destroy human life and dignity but by plunging into the midst of the struggle and by fully assuming it. Only churches which hold themselves accountable to their respective countries and to the righteousness—and peace—of the kingdom of God can offer a true contribution to the reconciliation of international conflicts.

My argument may seem to be one-sided. Should I not balance the picture by equally stressing the need for the "younger" churches to recognize the natural solidarity of churches in the developed world with the interests of their respective countries? As a matter of fact I cannot. We deal with a one-sided situation which can be met only in a one-sided way. This holds true in both international and inter-ecclesiastical relations. The existing injustice cannot be corrected by means of carefully balanced statements in which all parties pledge themselves to the same measure of sovereignty and dependence—as if the point of departure were the same. A handicap must be overcome, and it will be overcome only if whatever structures of world unity are developed lean heavily on the side of the restoration of selfhood to churches in the Third World. Otherwise, the only path to integrity left to them will be that of temporary withdrawal from all supranational or supraregional alliances.

3. What is "Methodism"? Particularly, how can Methodism understand itself regarding the question of a world community? I have already pointed out that it has a weak confessional consciousness in terms of doctrinal distinctiveness. Wesley seems to have been right when he said, "We hold no peculiar doctrine." Wherein, then, lies our peculiar genius? During the last few years I have heard some voices—not always coming from uninformed or unrepresentative people—attempting to make up for our lack of confessional distinctiveness by emphasizing our supposedly efficient organization. For some it is the connectional system of conferences, for others our form of episcopacy with its appointive power, for still others our itinerant ministry. Methodism may not have a profound theological legacy, but it is a tightly knit and efficient movement. If this is our point of entry into the question of a world movement, we may as well confess that we are peculiarly ill fitted to face constructively the challenge of the situation that I have endeavored to describe! It would simply prove that Methodism is tied to a structural model derived from (or concomitant with) the organizational patterns of big industry and corporations—a typical example of structures of domination and colonialism which must be viewed negatively in relation to our problem. Whatever merits this system may have had in the development of the Methodist churches, and whatever its suitability for particular circumstances, it seems to me that the unification from the top, the chain of command, and the principle of heteronomy

which permeate our present structures disqualify them for a world ecclesiastical family in our time.

The ability to institutionalize its missionary concern efficiently doubtless was a basic fact of the Methodist revival. But the sort of structural fundamentalism which now insists upon Methodist organization as our distinctive heritage commits a serious fallacy, namely mistaking a particular form of organization for the deep insight that found expression in it. This insight is that Christian fellowship and missionary impulse belong together and must find visible forms of realization and promotion. The heart of Wesley's ecclesiology, I would claim, is his creative yoking of an emphasis on the *koinonia* of believers with an emphasis on the missionary (evangelistic) character of their calling. He articulated this concept not so much in terms of doctrine as in terms of a cluster of structures (bands, classes, societies, conferences, itinerancy, lay preachers) which gave visible expression to his ecclesiological vision.[7] It seems to me that only a wooden and misplaced loyalty moves some Methodists today to insist on these particular structures as the *sine qua non* and infallible sacraments of the Methodist spirit. Quite to the contrary, it is our task to find in our particular situation, in view of our needs and possibilities, those structures which will best express and implement for our age the synthesis of the missional and *koinonial* dimensions of the Christian community. The heritage bequeathed by Wesley's organizational genius—which is indeed part of the Methodist vision—is a

[7] I have developed this point further in "Catholic and Protestant—But Missionary: Wesley's Explicit and Implicit Ecclesiology," *Journal: Methodist Theological School in Ohio*, VI (1968), 1-10.

thrust toward visibility, not the particular forms of visibility that he devised.

We can summarize this second step in our consideration by saying that it is the task of Methodism as a world movement to seek those forms of local and universal visibility which will best express, in a postconfessional and deeply divided world, the missional and *koinonial* calling of the people of God.

III

The last step in our presentation must attempt to draw some concrete consequences of the picture sketched in the earlier sections. I shall not, of course, undertake to draw the blueprint of a structure for world Methodism. But it may be useful to suggest some definite guidelines for any such structure.

1. We must think of a world Methodist structure as an executor of the Methodist heritage. I hasten to point out that such an executor has a double duty: to settle the inheritance, so that at the end of the process he puts himself out of business as executor; and to make sure that the legitimate heirs come into full possession of their share. Both sides of the task must be equally emphasized. There is no room for a permanent confessional structure, because the service long rendered by the denominations in preserving the manifoldness of the faith and furthering the mission of Christ must now find new channels more in accord with our age and circumstances. But we must be sure that the tradition, value, and experience which the Spirit of God has granted to the denominations are preserved in the new structures. We have no

right either to squander the inheritance or to keep it as if it were our own private possession.

It is not enough, however, to disclaim permanency for our confessional structures, meanwhile building them in such a way that—whether we plan it or not—they have an inbuilt tendency to self-perpetuation. What we know today about the self-perpetuating tendencies in all bureaucracies, the inertia of institutional forms, and the inherent expansionism of budgets should prompt us to take the measures necessary to ensure against these risks. Precariousness must be visible in the structures themselves and in their functioning. The agency that acts as executor must be devised according to its function: the mechanisms and the drive toward self-liquidation must be present from the very beginning.[8]

2. How can the inheritance be distributed? If we take seriously the conception of catholicity as the presence of "all in each place" (to use the felicitous expression coined at the New Delhi World Council Assembly), our concern must be to ensure that the insights and resources of the whole of Methodism—in its historical and geographical extension—are made available, on the one hand, to the general ecumenical dialogue and, on the other, to each national and regional Methodist church, *according to the local conditions.* This makes several requirements of us: (a) Means must be made available and occasions created for the study of our experience

---

[8] It occurs to me that one way to help in this direction would be to "rotate" the seat of such a world Methodist structure. The fact that such rotation would be all the more cumbersome the greater the agency grew would perhaps be its greatest asset. The difficulty of effecting such rotation, particularly when the seat falls in the Third World, would also help us to measure the distance between a centralizing structure and a world structure.

and historical heritage.[9] (b) We must recognize the existence of different patterns and rhythms in the movement toward a postconfessional situation (some churches primarily in process of extension, some entering the road of cooperation, some engaged in union negotiations, etc.); consequently we must also recognize that the kinds and amounts of assistance that can and should be given to the churches are to be regulated by these different rhythms and patterns. (c) Both the amount of influence carried by and the use made of the assistance must be determined by those receiving it, not by those giving it. This requires a structure of consultation and accountability rather than one of legislation and execution. The world Methodist structure must be the place where Methodist or Methodist-related churches can ask questions and have them debated, request specific "services," and explain to each other (in terms related to their common heritage) the things they are doing; it must not be the place from which they receive legally binding decisions on doctrine, polity, or planning. (d) Communications, which so far have followed almost exclusively a line of convergence on British and American centers, must be rerouted so that a multiple net of communication replaces the "central" one which today standardizes everything into a single language and a single code. Is it not abnormal that, so far at least, Portuguese-speaking African Methodists and Spanish-speaking Latin

---

[9] This hardly requires an elaborate mechanism; it would be enough to continue some such gathering as the Oxford Institute on Methodist Theological Studies and to establish ways of disseminating information about work done by Methodist theologians and Methodist-related schools. Such people and institutions could also be called upon to conduct—within the framework of their regular work—study or research on issues important for some or all Methodist churches.

American Methodists (to name one among many cases) have met only in England or the United States and in circumstances in which the agenda of their consultation was set by the concerns and needs of the British and American Methodist churches?

3. We have mentioned "services" for which particular churches could apply. I am thinking here not only of "consultation" in which common problems or problems peculiar to some area or region are freely shared and discussed by all, which should be one of the basic functions of a world Methodist structure, but also of "technical problems" in which the resources of different Methodist churches can be placed at the service of any one of them. Here are some examples of such service:

A. A church in Africa is facing the problem of massive internal migrations; a team from Indonesia and Brazil can help it study the situation and plan its approach to the problem.

B. Methodists in Argentina and Uruguay are negotiating union with Baptist and Reformed Churches; consultation with Methodists in Ceylon and Australia can help them see the way to articulate the Methodist heritage in such a union.

C. An American anthropologist and a British sociologist are sent to Bolivia (on the request of the Bolivian church) to be part of a team studying the adaptation of the Methodist Church there to the conditions of different geographic and ethnic areas.

D. A group of economists and sociologists from Methodist churches in the Third World sits for a month with staff of the National Division of the Board of Missions of The United Methodist Church to plan an educational program for Methodist college students or Methodist businessmen regarding Christian responsibility for international relations.[10]

4. It could be pointed out that most of the activities described immediately above, and indeed most of what is suggested in previous paragraphs, can be done just as well or even better interdenominationally. This is true. They should be so done wherever the ecumenical "rhythm" of the churches makes it possible. But in certain cases it must still be done as an activity of the office of the "executor" of the confessional heritage. The important point in such cases is that it be done in such a way that the rhythm is quickened in the direction of postconfessionalism. How, then, can these churches be involved in study and action with non-Methodist sister churches through the services and consultation provided by world Methodism? How can this be done without maneuvering the churches or bribing them into a relation which does not spring from their own existence and experience? These objectives can be accomplished only when consultations and services help the ecumenically "underdeveloped" churches to consider and analyze their own life and mission in such a way that *they* themselves come to understand the ecumenical imperative of their own situation.

---

[10] These examples have been confined to specific, short-range projects. I have elsewhere discussed the question of local (national) vs. central (international) planning in relation to the provision of missionary personnel and funds. Cf. "Missionary Planning and National Integrity," *Christianity and Crisis*, XXVIII (1968), 140-43.

Let us be aware, at the same time, that a church is ecumenically "underdeveloped" not only when is not seeking union with others, but also when it has lost its missionary and evangelistic passion, or when it has settled into rigid traditions (whether its own or supposedly ecumenical ones) and fails to face the challenge of the *oikoumene*—the inhabited world in all its cultural variety (youth, the underprivileged, the new world of science, etc.). To help a church involve itself ecumenically is to help it see itself actively engaged on all these frontiers. If this is so, it is not a question of some churches moving others to an ecumenical maturity which the former already have achieved, but of all helping each other to discover the full meaning of their own ecumenical maturity.

5. Finally, we seek ecumenically the forms that make visible the *una sancta*, the structures of universal Christian relationship for today. We are increasingly realizing that such forms are not extant somewhere in past history or preserved intact today by any one tradition. They must be discovered and worked out in the historical junctures of our time. The experience gained in the provisional structures of world Methodism may help provide sketches and drafts of the kind of world ecumenical structures which will help the Christian churches in our time make visible their worldwide fellowship. The very fact of the provisionality of the kind of world structure that we have suggested, combined with the emphasis on consultation, accountability, and mutual service, rather than legislation and jurisdiction, may help break a concept of church unity too unilaterally shaped by the juridical status of established churches and point to a new conception and realization of universal church unity.

It seems to me that the Christian churches and the ecumenical movement are baffled today because they have caught the vision of their unity in Christ and have discovered the imperative to service but cannot devise the structures for expressing and implementing their vision. The peculiar contribution of Methodism does not lie in the creation of an imposing world church which can successfully "negotiate" unity from a position of strength. It more likely lies in proclaiming and illustrating the truth of the world as parish—as that endless variety of concrete places where the fellowship of believers finds appropriate visible expression in missionary service.

v
british methodism's ecumenical stance today

The Christian church is divided in every country where the Christian religion has taken root, except for those in which a particular form of Christianity, usually the Roman Catholic one, so dominates the scene that no other form is tolerated or possible. But each country has its own pattern of divisions, and in no country is the pattern exactly the same as it is in any other. This is why ecumenical discussion across national borders is such a difficult and delicate business.

Such discussion should be carried out in depth, or not carried out at all. For in a superficial discussion it is fatally easy for all participants to read their own situations into the words of their interlocutors, especially when the actual words and phrases used in the different countries are identical, though their connotations and overtones are vastly different. The word "Baptist" means quite different things in the United States, and indeed in different parts of the United States, in Britain, and in Russia. "Methodism" means something quite different to an Anglican in Britain from what it means to a Lutheran in Germany. And the imagination boggles at the effort to understand the various meanings of the word "Anglican" in various parts of the world; for in England itself the Church of England means a hundred different things. A sympathetic observer of the Church of England finds it very hard to say what the Church of England is; a member of the Church of England finds it impossible, because his views are hopelessly colored by the part of that church in which he happens to be. The various brands of Anglicanism have been exported to many other parts of the world, so that each English-speaking country has its own brand, colonialized or indigenized, and not even the recent Lambeth Conference of bishops of the Anglican Communion could nullify or conceal that fact.

The pattern of divisiveness in every country is largely the product of that country's history, just as the program of ecumenism, if it is to be successful, must conform to that history as it is continued into the present day. Nowhere is that fact more true than in Britain. It is impossible to understand what is happening in that country in the matter of church relations without some knowledge of its history. The history to which I refer is not by any means simply ecclesiastical history, though it is with the latter that this essay must be mostly concerned. Politics, economics, and sociology are equally important constituents and in some periods much more important than what was actually happening in the church.

We cannot here go back to the beginnings, even if we could say exactly what those beginnings were. About the late medieval church in England we must, however, say that it was probably no better and no worse, either in theology or practice, than the church on the continent of Europe, save that it suffered some disadvantage culturally and derived some advantage ethically from its geographical position. That position had helped for centuries to give the English monarchy a sturdy independence of papal suzerainty, and when Henry VIII repudiated his country's allegiance to the pope, most observers thought of the event as simply another in the long series of English cockings of the snook at Rome, as recurrent as wars in the Middle East or revolutions in some Latin American republics today.

In fact, Henry's action was much more important than anything which had happened before, and it marked the final break with Rome. But it was very far from turning England into a Protestant country. In one sense this has never happened. The principles of the Lutheran or the Calvinist Reformation have never been thoroughly applied to the Church of England, except for a brief and unsuccessful period during the Civil Wars which, as we shall see, made it unlikely that those principles would ever be brought to bear again. Henry VIII left the church free of Roman control and of certain of the cruder superstitions that had held it up to the ridicule of the humanists, but it remained Roman in doctrine and largely Roman in practice. Henry's successor was Edward VI, and his unscrupulous advisers (he himself never reached the fullness of royal age and authority) tried to carry out a Continental-type Reformation for their own reasons before they lost their power. They worked fast but not fast enough, though they did enable Cranmer to produce the permanent treasure of the *Book of Common Prayer*. The king's early death brought in Mary and the reinstatement of the "old religion." Mary was so inept and bigotedly cruel in the execution of her policy that she made England safe for Protestantism, perhaps forever. But even the reaction against her, which set in as soon as she died and which Elizabeth I exploited with consummate skill, did not inaugurate a total reform of the Church of England.

The Elizabethan Settlement, as Elizabeth's arrangements are optimistically called, was an ingenious compromise that did not quite succeed, an attempt at comprehensiveness which fell far short of comprehending. Perhaps her task was impossible. She wished primarily to unite the nation against its probable aggressors, and this, she thought, could not be done without religious unity (she was wrong at this point, for Roman Catholics joined with Protestants to defeat the Spanish Armada). So she conceived and brought into existence a church somewhat reformed, generously vague in doctrine, moderately catholic in rites, ceremonies, and vestments, and replete with a full episcopal hierarchy. This church she supported to the limit with finance and prestige, while retaining the appointment of its dignitaries in her own hands. To her delight it was greeted by her beneficiaries as the "middle way" between Rome and Geneva, and asserted to be based on the triple foundation of Scripture, tradition, and sound reason. Surely, they thought, this was the church to which every Englishman, aware of the dangers of fanaticism and of any extreme view on religion, proud of his emancipation from the foreign power of the Bishop of Rome, and apprehensive of the disasters which threatened a divided country, would be enthusiastically eager to belong. And, indeed, since then this has been the church to which most Englishmen *have* wished to belong, or since "belonging to a church" has come to imply rather more in the way of personal commitment than the average Englishman is willing to countenance, the church of which most Englishmen have been willing to make use for the purposes of baptisms, marriages, and funerals.

Most, but by no means all; the minority of dissenters from established Christianity has in every age included a considerable number of those to whom Christianity is a matter of deep personal concern and involvement. The danger of dissent was built into the Elizabethan Settlement. For where was the place in the sober and decorous parish churches of town and countryside for the biblical doctrines of justification by faith alone, the priesthood of all believers, the sole authority of Scripture, the divine election before time began of the saints and the reprobates? Not that these doctrines were ruled out by Anglicanism, but they were hushed, muted, and on the way to being forgotten—or so it was thought or suspected by those who wished for "reformation without tarrying for any"; they had "tarried" long enough, and now Elizabeth's regime opened up a further indefinite period of "tarrying." The Independents and Baptists could not bear to stay in the Church of England at all; the Presbyterians could bear to stay only so long as they could hope to obtain by subversion from within what had not been granted by legislation from without.

Elizabeth's strong statesmanship contained these dissident elements, though not without difficulty and repression. The Stuarts, enamored of the divine right which a curious understanding of Reformed theology had ascribed to them, and badly overplaying the hand which was thus dealt out to them, made armed conflict inevitable once the economic and political grievances were added to the religious ones. Yet the Puritans, who were the natural enemies of the Stuarts and who prevailed for a short time, had no chance of ultimate success, for English people as a whole do not wish religion to affect their private lives except in the most gentle and courteous way. After their downfall, the Restoration showed that the Stuarts and the bishops had learned nothing and forgotten nothing. The possibility of the breakup of the English nation into two had been inherent in English life since the time of Henry. Charles II, and more particularly the advisers on whom he depended for money, turned this possibility into an actuality which they proceeded to canonize and perpetuate.

Thus the group called the Dissenters or Nonconformists became second-class citizens and second-class Christians, and in spite of the very gradual easement of their religious, social, and political condition (they looked after their economic easement for themselves), they have to some extent remained so until this day. There are still large and influential spheres of English life, mostly secular, where to be an Anglican (practicing or merely traditional) is the only really acceptable thing, and Nonconformists are regarded as awkward or agreeable oddities. Hence was developed that "consciousness of effortless superiority" once aptly ascribed to members of my Oxford college, Balliol, which has marked bishops, priests, deacons, and members of the Church of England from time almost immemorial, and still confuses ecumenical relations except in those enlightened Anglican circles where men and women have come to terms with it and overcome it.

But it must not be supposed from this that the Church of England has gone triumphantly forward from strength to strength from the base of its firm and entrenched position. On the contrary, the departure of the Nonconformists in the seventeenth century robbed it of many of its most devout members. A further bloodletting occurred when the Nonjurors, a small group of catholic-minded bishops and theologians, left the Church of England in the early seventeenth century. The worst loss of all occurred when the Methodist revival withdrew the majority of those who were evangelically inclined. It did not withdraw all of these, of course; the Calvinistic wing of the Evangelicals remained staunchly Anglican and infused into the Church of England much of the spiritual vigor which still remained at the beginning of the nineteenth century. But by the end of the first quarter of the new century Anglican Evangelicalism was a spent force, except among a few closely knit groups which have survived until the present day and have in recent years burst into surprisingly new life. The Church of England was certainly in danger in the 1830's, not so much from the intrusion of the state, as the Tractarians maintained (for the state was clumsily trying to reform the church), but from the steady growth of Methodism and Dissent, from its own disinterest in the fate of the industrial masses, and from the inertia which breeds corruption. John Henry Newman and his friends carried out a large-scale rescue operation of lasting importance, so successful that it survived Newman's own defection to Rome and gave a vitality and color to a dying church, on which vitality, in no small measure, it still lives today. The triumph of Anglo-Catholic theology, with its undue emphasis on episcopal succession and patristic doctrines, in universities, seminaries, and parishes, was partly due to the absence of any other Anglican theology to compete with it. Evangelical theology could never capture more than the few, and biblical criticism subjected it to a process of steady erosion; Continental theology was unknown. Anglo-Catholicism held the field. Many British Methodists think it still holds the field, so pervasive was its influence for so long. In actual fact, it has now considerably declined, though many incumbents in outlying parishes still cling to it as the last refuge against radicalism and ecumenism. Responsible Anglican theologians today were mostly brought up on it, but they have now abandoned its extremes and its exclusiveness.

Where does Methodism stand in relation to this historical

process? It fits into neither the Anglican nor the Dissenter category. It forms a category of its own. In the words of an early Anglican-Methodist report, it "lies athwart" the Anglican and Dissenting traditions. It took its birth in an episcopal context and has never repudiated episcopacy. It assumed from the start the truths of orthodox Anglicanism, adding only its desire that some of its forgotten doctrines should be taken out of store and re-presented. It accepted the sober dignity of the *Book of Common Prayer*, asking permission to introduce the power of preaching and the refreshment of hymn singing into its carefully ordered ritual. So far, it represented Anglicanism with its feeling heightened and its religion made more personal—and with the attendant dangers of enthusiasm and disorder. But separation from the Church of England and rapid growth in the new industrialized, highly self-approving Britain of the nineteenth century subjected it to all kinds of different influences and encouraged it to create and develop an ethos, a worship, and a structure of its own. Its natural allies were now the other Free Churches, and throughout the nineteenth century it went increasingly away from the Church of England and nearer to Nonconformity. As the Church of England under Tractarian influence seemed to be drifting toward Catholic practices and beliefs, and to be well on the way back to Rome, Wesleyan Methodism began to cast itself, not with complete improbability, in the role of the Protestant church of Britain, while the smaller Methodist churches (such as the Primitive Methodists and the Bible Christians), which had broken away from their parent body on the grounds of its excessive conformity to the usages of the past, made no bones about calling themselves Nonconformists. Nineteenth-century Britain was far too successful and individualistic to think in terms of church union; but if the Wesleyan Methodists had ever contemplated such a thing, it would have been toward the other Free Churches that it would have turned, willing at this stage to jettison its Anglican heritage without a murmur.

Free Church union did in fact attract the attention of some Methodist and other Free Church leaders during the years immediately before the First World War, but no determined effort to launch such a project was ever really made, and, indeed, whenever the matter has been mentioned, the insistence of Baptists—or rather of a powerful group of Baptists—on the necessity of "believers' baptism" has always stood effectively in the way. Thus, in 1910, when the Edinburgh Conference is usually thought to have launched the ecumenical movement, the situation in Britain could hardly have been less favorable than it was for its acceptance and furtherance. On the one side was the Church of England, established in every sense, proud and privileged, socially and culturally exalted, taking its stand on a theology which justified on the highest possible ground the contempt of Nonconformity which it entertained anyway on historical grounds. On the other side were the various Free Churches, Wesleyan Methodism the strongest and most invulnerably bourgeois, all of them pledged to the doctrines of individual salvation and incurably suspicious of Anglican claims and achievements, and willing to take over the evangelism and education of the nation as soon as the Church of England stepped down, or was forced to step down, from its position of undeserved eminence. The transformation of the entire scene which has taken place since then is nothing short of miraculous, and those of us who are sometimes frustrated by the slowness

of ecumenical progress need constantly to remind ourselves
of this fact. But, of course, the forces which made unity
impossible in 1910 still operate in a modified and domesticated form to make it difficult today.

British Methodism, for reasons which should now be plain,
was not immediately swept up into the ecumenical movement, though Scott Lidgett, its one ecumenical statesman
of that period, was saying before 1910 that the church's
divisions robbed it of catholicity and, not much later, that
denominationalism was dead. By 1925, the Wesleyan Methodist Church joined in the negotiations for church union in
South India and is said to have added a drive and purpose
to the proceedings which had previously not been very evident. Methodist union in Great Britain followed in 1932.
The reincorporation of the "Nonconformist" Methodist
bodies, those of the Primitive Methodists and the United
Methodists, with the Wesleyan Methodists in the "Methodist Church of Great Britain" cannot be said to have made reunion with the Church of England easier, and it may well be
that without Methodist union there would already be a
union between the Wesleyan Methodists and the Church
of England. But it would not have been right for the Wesley-
ans to turn away from their Primitive and United brethren
even for that.

The bishops of the Anglican Communion, assembled in
Lambeth in 1920, had meanwhile issued an "Appeal to all
Christian People" to reunite Christendom on the fourfold
basis of Bible, creeds, sacraments, and a universally acceptable, i.e. an episcopal, ministry; and the representatives of
all the churches in Britain, including the Methodist ones,
had discussed the "Appeal" at length. But no progress that

was made had much impact on the life or thinking of Methodists at large, and the whole matter remained in the realm of the theoretical and academic throughout the interwar period. In the Student Christian Movement some of us were learning to look beyond our own denominations to the coming great church of the future, and a group of Cambridge theological students to which I belonged met in a village church on Ascension Day each year to pray for unity. As a result of careful conversations a *Scheme for a United Church* was published in 1939, but the Second World War engulfed us all before it could be properly discussed, and it has since been forgotten.

In 1946 something really got started. Dr. Geoffrey Fisher, then Archbishop of Canterbury, preached a sermon in Cambridge which suggested that the Free Churches should enter into communion with the Church of England by taking episcopacy, by which he meant *historic* episcopacy, into their system. Dr. Fisher did not intend that such a step should be a preparation for full organic union; he was content, and he still is content, that the churches in Britain should remain separate from each other, as long as they have full sacramental communion with each other. We shall see that those who pursued his suggestion were not similarly content. In recent years, having retired from the archbishopric but having retained his physical and intellectual energy, he has made frequent and unwelcome sallies into the arena which he has officially relinquished. He has urged his successor to carry out what he, Dr. Fisher, proposed and not a tittle more—like a retired headmaster telling his successor how to run his school, or the inventor of the first airplane trying to prevent the development of the supersonic airliner. We must defend his consistency and the importance of his first initiative, though we deplore his interference in something which is not now within his area of responsibility.

The tide has flowed past Dr. Fisher. The first step resulting from his Cambridge sermon was a general conference of the denominations which developed the implications of his suggestion. This conference concluded, among other things, that the way forward was for individual denominations to enter, if they wished, into direct negotiations with the Church of England. This was accepted as the right procedure in view of the different historical and theological relationships of the various churches to that church. But only the Presbyterian Churches of Scotland and England and the Methodist Church of Great Britain took up the proposal. This fact needs to be pointed out, since both Methodists and Presbyterians have been charged with getting into a private huddle with the Church of England and forgetting their Free Church brethren. For reasons which seemed to them to be sufficient the other Free Churches did not feel at that time able to pursue the matter, nor have they done so since (except that the Congregationalists are in an advanced state of negotiation with the Presbyterians, not the Anglicans). The Methodist Church professed its readiness to enter into direct conversations with the Church of England on three strict understandings: (a) The division to be healed was not a division of the Methodists from the church of Christ, but a division *within* the church of Christ of two churches from each other. (b) No specific doctrine of episcopacy was to be pressed on the Methodists if and when they took episcopacy into their system. (c) The relations of communion with the other Methodist bodies of the world and the other Free

Churches in Britain which the British Methodist Church enjoyed were to be retained at all stages in the development of union with the Church of England. It was seen that the last proviso especially would be difficult to honor, but the Methodists made their insistence on it clear from the outset. They have not retracted it at any point since, nor have they done so with the other provisos.

These conditions were accepted by the Church of England, and official conversations began in 1956. It soon became apparent to those engaged in them that to aim at less than full organic union between the two churches was not sufficient by biblical or theological standards. The notion of a permanent juxtaposition of two churches in full communion with each other but exercising separate spiritual jurisdictions in the same geographical area and among the same people, infringed the New Testament conception of the church in any one place as being the church for all in the one place; and it did not seem possible, on a coherent theology of the church, to have in perpetuity two bishops, albeit in communion with each other, each of them acting as bishop of the place in which they both lived. Thus the *Interim Statement* of the conversations between the Church of England and the Methodist Church came out strongly in favor of accepting organic union as the goal to be sought, and sketched a scheme by which the objective could be reached in two stages.[1] The Anglican bishops, meeting at Lambeth in 1958—as it happened under the presidency of Dr. Fisher—strongly approved of organic union as the goal to be sought, and both churches

---

[1] *Conversations between the Church of England and the Methodist Church: An Interim Statement 1958* (London: SPCK and Epworth Press, 1958).

encouraged the Joint Commission to work out its proposed scheme in detail.

In 1963 the Commission's *Report* set out a full-fledged scheme of union.[2] It proposed that the first stage, that of full communion without union, should be inaugurated by a Service of Reconciliation and by the consecration of Methodist bishops in the historic succession. A draft of the Service of Reconciliation was published in the *Report*. Its four main items were two acts in which the peoples of each church were received into the membership of the other, and two acts in which the ministry of each church was received into the ministry of the other. The two ministerial acts contained prayers in each case for the gifts of the Holy Spirit which would make possible the larger ministry into which each group of ministers was to enter; then came the laying on of hands in silence, first by bishops on the heads of Methodist ministers, then by Methodist ministers on the heads of Anglican bishops and priests. The service was to culminate in the joint celebration of Holy Communion.

The rest of the *Report* dealt with theological and practical problems raised by differences between the two churches, suggesting that there would be a greater upheaval for the Methodists at stage one, and a greater upheaval for the Church of England at stage two. It insisted that there was no doctrinal difference between the churches sufficient to make union impossible or even difficult; but it made clear that the unofficial Methodist practice of inviting to Holy Communion "all who love the Lord Jesus" and the giving of

[2] *Conversations between the Church of England and the Methodist Church: A Report to the Archbishops of Canterbury and York and the Conference of the Methodist Church* (London: Church Information Office and Epworth Press, 1963).

dispensations to Methodist laymen to administer the sacrament of Holy Communion could not continue long into stage one.

The publication of the *Report* initiated a period of sharp controversy, especially in the Methodist Church. It was evident from the start that the majority of theological teachers and chief administrators in this church favored the scheme as statesmanlike and consistent with Methodist belief and practice, even though they admitted that the introduction of episcopacy would bring about basic changes in Methodist structure and precipitate the loss of certain practices dear to many Methodists. But they had no doubt that biblical truth, a true doctrine of the church, and the needs of the age combined to make this scheme, or one very like it, the right way forward for Methodism. There was considerable opposition, some of it theological, most of it emotional. The *Report* itself contained a minority report from four Methodists, and the leading theologian among the four, Professor C. Kingsley Barrett of Durham, led the small band of Methodist theologians who held that episcopacy was ruled out by Scripture, and that the Service of Reconciliation, together with the requirement that all new Methodist ministers thereafter be episcopally ordained, implied that Methodist ministers had not received a true ordination within the Methodist Church. The rest of the opposition came from those who could not bear the thought that the Methodism they knew was about to be changed forever, and who feared (as perhaps every British Methodist was tempted, however unworthily, at some time or other to fear) that the whole scheme was a concealed takeover bid by the Church of England—a view which I have seen expressed in some less well-informed American periodicals. And, naturally, the traditional nonconformity and suspicion of the Established Church cherished by some sections of the Methodist Church led many otherwise well-disposed people into opposition.

But in 1965, when the *Report* was voted upon in the Anglican Convocations and the Methodist Conference, there was found to be a very large majority in each case willing to approve the scheme in principle. There is reason for thinking that the support among the rank and file of the ministry and laity, and in the case of Methodism, especially of the laity, was not as great as the majorities in the higher courts of the churches suggested; but each church had followed its proper constitutional procedure. A new Unity Commission was at once established to revise the scheme where necessary, to clarify a large number of points which had caused difficulty in the period of argument and controversy, and to produce a new ordinal for use in both churches from the start of stage one.

The Unity Commission had an even bigger job on hand than it knew when it began. It heard all the objections to the Service of Reconciliation, and it made a number of alterations chiefly designed to allay Methodist fears. It modeled the draft ordinal on South Indian lines, and made the startling proposal (startling, that is, in England) that ordinands should be ordained "presbyters," not "priests" or "ministers."

The rest of its interim report, *Towards Reconciliation*,[3] published in 1967, was devoted to showing that on doctrinal

[3] *Towards Reconciliation: The Interim Statement of the Anglican-Methodist Unity Commission* (London: SPCK and Epworth Press, 1967).

issues there was certainly enough agreement for the two churches to unite, since the differences were inside the churches rather than across them. Particularly important was its argument that the Service of Reconciliation *could* be interpreted by those who wished to do so as conferring ordination on Methodist ministers, but that there was *nothing whatever* in the service to require this interpretation, and that the transcending purpose of the ministerial part of the service was that each church should submit its ministry to God and share it with the other.

The interim report was judged especially helpful by the Methodists, among whom it won a number of doubters to the scheme. But in the Church of England the effect was different. It brought Lord Fisher, who was afraid that the peculiar character of the Church of England was in danger, into battle against the scheme; and a group of Anglo-Catholics, who had apparently realized with belated suddenness that the Methodist Church was not being absorbed into the Church of England and was not gladly accepting the ordination of its ordained ministers, made known a number of violent objections. They suggested that the permission to hold more than one doctrine smacked of theological irresponsibility—forgetting that the Church of England *lives* by being comprehensive—and they also audibly trembled for the ark of the covenant in the form of the catholic doctrine of the priesthood. The Unity Commission heard representatives of all the objectors and all their points of view; it discovered that each group of objectors favored a scheme of unity which was wholly unacceptable to every other group. It therefore went ahead with the further refinement and improvement of the existing scheme, and published its final report in two parts early in 1968.[4]

This *Report* shows the marks made by the Anglo-Catholic objectors who had said that the new ordinal expressed a noncatholic doctrine of the ministry. To meet this objection, certain changes were made which do not offend the Methodists, and a careful statement on the nature of the ministry, approved by Roman Catholic and Free Church observers as well as by the unanimous vote of the Commission—a quite miraculous unanimity on so delicate a matter—appears in the preface to the revised draft ordinal. Methodists assert their belief in the priesthood of all believers, and Anglo-Catholics suspect that this belief implies a denial of any proper doctrine of an ordained priesthood. These paragraphs seek to meet this point:

The royal priesthood which the whole Church has received from Christ her Lord, and in which each member of the Body shares, is exercised by the faithful in different ways. The distinctive Ministry is a special form of this participation. It is in this way that the priesthood of bishop and presbyter should be understood.

The Ministry is thus a divinely appointed organ which acts in relation to the whole Body in the name of Christ and which represents the priestly service of the whole Body in its common worship. Ministers are, as the Methodist *Statement on Ordination* says, both Christ's ambassadors and the representatives of the whole people of God.[5]

---

[4] *Anglican-Methodist Unity: Report of the Anglican-Methodist Unity Commission. I. The Ordinal. II. The Scheme* (London: SPCK and Epworth Press, 1968).

[5] *Anglican-Methodist Unity: I. The Ordinal*, p. 12.

The word "presbyter" is adhered to. For the rest, the *Report* deals with problems such as open communion, marriage discipline, and the future functions of Methodist bishops. It calls on the churches to enter stage one "with the firm and declared intention" to retain existing relations with other churches at all stages of the union. It also reasserts the "open" —or some would say "ambiguous"—nature of the Service of Reconciliation and revises that service in such a way as to make clearer than ever that this act is not just a bringing together of the ministries: it is primarily the coming together of the *peoples* of both churches for the supreme task of mission. Furthermore, after examining all alternative proposals for the union of the churches, the *Report* states the Commission's considered and profound conviction that there is no other way forward than the way it proposes, and that this is the right way.

It should be noted that the *Report* does not propose the separation of the future united church from the state, but it does propose considerable amendments of the present relationships between church and state in England.

I must say that I do not recognize in the united English church of the future the remotest resemblance to the kind of national church feared by some American Methodists. We utterly repudiate state control; we have no desire of uniformity—rather we aim at a "saving diversity" within unity, a much wider diversity than Methôdism itself can ever provide, but a unity in which the Methodist ideals of a religious society and of personal commitment to Christ find their place and find themselves within a larger whole.

The Unity Commission had to record one dissentient vote, that of Dr. James Packer, an Anglican Conservative-Evangelical, who could not see the necessity for a Service of Reconciliation, though he accepted every other part of the scheme.

The whole matter is now before the churches for their decision, and this decision must be made in the very near future. If it is made in the right direction, the Service of Reconciliation could take place early in 1971. Other ecumenical issues are, of course, also in the air. The Presbyterian and Congregational Churches in England are hoping for an organic union by 1970. Conversations between the Church of England and the Church of Scotland are slowly making progress. And many churches, including the Methodist Church, have started discussions with Roman Catholics on various matters, though there is no talk of union. In 1964 the non-Roman British churches were called by the famous Nottingham Faith and Order Conference to make a covenant for union by a stated date, and they suggested that this date should be Easter Sunday, 1980. The Methodist Church has expressed its wholehearted willingness to take part in this as an earnest of its intention that Anglican-Methodist union should be the first step to a much larger union. But the issue on which practically everything else depends is the Anglican-Methodist one. If the scheme is turned down, there will be widespread disillusionment and disintegration in both churches—but also far beyond them. It is hard to see how English Christianity could recover from such a blow to its credit and its claim to have a message for the nation. The discouragement to many of the most forward-looking members of both churches would be crippling. These forward-looking people are not only people at the top; in fact they are far more ministers and lay people working in local situations experimentally and ecumenically and pinning their

127

hopes on a union between their churches. Anglican-Methodist union is not imposed from above. The movement from above is being met halfway by yet more vigorous movement from below.

But what shall we do if the scheme breaks down? I suppose we may turn to the other Free Churches; but to work for unity in their direction, and leave the Anglicans, will be to perpetuate that very rift in English church life which the whole movement is designed to heal. Some might even urge us to turn to a world Methodist church, but this holds little attraction for English Methodists.

If the Anglican-Methodist union scheme fails, perhaps we shall stop church unity efforts and hand things over to the secular ecumenists. I wholeheartedly approve of the secular ecumenists who say let us get this business of church unity settled quickly so we can get on to something else. But we cannot just hand things over to them, for they derive their strength and inspiration from the other kind of ecumenism, and without it they might well be forced to stop in their tracks. Surely the right thing is for the two kinds of ecumenism to remain in dialogue, for each needs the other.

It is by no means certain that the scheme will go through. In the Methodist Church the opposition is vigorous, but probably not very powerful among those who have to make the decision. Dr. Barrett retains his theological objections, with a diminishing number of supporters. The organization self-styled the "Voice of Methodism" speaks noisily, but for only a small section of Methodism. The real danger to the scheme, it must be frankly admitted, is from the Anglican side. A large number of Conservative-Evangelicals may follow Dr. Packer's lead and reject the scheme because it contains a Service of Reconciliation. The right-wing Anglo-Catholics may reject it for precisely the opposite reason—because the Service of Reconciliation is not explicitly an ordination of Methodist ministers. The hope of reunion in England may founder on an unholy alliance of these two groups. We are working very hard to prevent this disastrous culmination. And I believe that we may succeed. The bishops of the Anglican Communion meeting in August, 1968, approved the Service of Reconciliation by a very large majority. So we are becoming hopeful. But the issue is a crucial one. For at this point our ecumenical aims are taken up into the whole question of the church's existence in the last third of the twentieth century. If the church's existence depends on the renewal of its mission, and if unity is bound up with renewal —and these propositions are undoubtedly true—we must go forward into unity as soon as possible, or the chance of renewal and mission will be taken from us. And who will be to blame but English Christians of the 1960's?

vi
methodism and the ecumenical movement: an asian perspective

My commitment to the ecumenical movement was first really made at the 1935 General Committee meeting of the World's Student Christian Federation in Sofia, Bulgaria. I had always been interested in interdenominational work and, since my Bangalore days when I was studying for the ministry, had also become interested in the church union movement as such. What made the WSCF meeting memorable was that I saw there, for the first time, what the ecumenical movement is about. The chairman of the Federation, Francis P. Miller, in his opening address spoke of "the church becoming visible." He emphasized the reality of the church as it is in God's plan and purpose, accented the truth that the church is not just an ideal to be sought but actually exists among and because of the Christian community, and then challenged us to participate responsibly in making this church more visible and recognizable in our day and generation.

I saw that the ecumenical movement cannot be equated either with interdenominational work or with negotiations for church union. These are aspects of a much larger undertaking. To make the church visible means to make it visible in society—in man's struggle for humanity and his search for God. The church, as a social organism, must become visibly a part of the total human enterprise. To make the church visible means also that its marks of unity, holiness, catholicity, and apostolicity should find relevant and effective manifestation in the lives and beliefs of Christians in community.

The ecumenical stance of Methodism should therefore,

in the first place, involve the dedication of Methodists to make their church visible as church. It is one thing for there to be a Methodist church and quite another thing for the Methodist church to be recognized as part of "the becoming visible" of the church. Today, in Asia especially, we are living in the midst of a far-reaching revolution which is at different stages in the different countries of Asia; and which, in each Asian country, is manifesting a different emphasis and witnessing to a different priority. In some countries the dominant movement is toward a more egalitarian society. In other countries the emphasis falls on a confrontation between religious revivalism and scientific secularism. In still other countries the search is for more responsible forms of government—government which is both competent and broad based. If the church is to become visible, it must become visible within this revolution. There must be participation by Christians in the revolution sweeping over their countries, as there must also be signs of the revolution's impact on the structures of the churches themselves.

Methodism was born during a period of revolution in the West. The Industrial Revolution in England was the context within which it grew, and in the New World it coincided with what may be called the first challenge to colonialism. John Wesley was driven by circumstance to work outside the Established Church's authority and to create a Christian community outside the mores of the middle class of his time. In the New World, Methodism provided the form of the church for men living on a moving frontier. It showed the marks of a movement rather than an establishment.

It is not possible to say that today the Methodist churches are proving that their origins are still a living heritage. Indeed, in many ways, the very success of Methodism, in establishing itself and in extending its size and prestige, has proved a sad deterrent to its becoming once again a movement. A few years ago, a poem by Peter Dickinson appeared in *Punch*, the well-known magazine published in England:

> Seek the goals our fathers sought!
> Fight the fights our granfers fought!
> Think the thoughts Keir Hardie thought!
>   Smite the ancient foe!
>
> Scorn all talk of change, for what
> Is innovation but a plot
> To move the battle to a spot
>   Which we do not know?
>
> Heavy armour shields each mind
> Forwards, sideways and behind.
> Though it makes us somewhat blind
>   We are used to that.
>
> When the harsh spectators swear
> That the real fight's elsewhere,
> That our blows smite empty air,
>   Let us still stand pat!
>
> Comrades, let us slay anew
> Dragon Great-grandfather slew
> That's what we're equipped to do.
>   That is all we know.
>
> Comrades, as our foes of late
> Have been far from adequate
> Targets for our ancient hate,
> Rather than come up to date
>   Let's invent a foe! [1]

[1] "Battle Song," March 31, 1965, © *Punch*.

This poem says simply and aptly what I have heard said countless times by Christians in so many discussions and in so many ways, and not least of all by Methodists.

Let us take note, then, that until and unless the ecumenical movement is seen as an attempt on the part of all the churches to make the church visible in the affairs of men, specific questions concerning interdenominational work and church union will remain purely technical questions dealing with the technical problems of form and structure, without dealing with the essential question of the mission of the church and its God-given function in the movement of human history. The church is a consequence and an instrument of God's mission as it is fulfilled within and upon his total creation. Once this connection between the being of the church and the mission of God is lost, the church is nothing more than a form of human community, even though it is a religious community. As such, its life and forms become determined purely sociologically.

This having been said, let us look at some of the specific topics implied in the title of this essay.

1. The Methodist Family

The Methodist church is one church throughout the world. The "people called Methodists" are one people. But there are important differences of opinion concerning the implications of this fact for world Methodism. Let me state my own conviction.

The common life is lived in terms of unities that are provided by the secular. The primary unity is that of the family. The worshiping life of the family is part of its common life. Those who live together worship together. The village congregation that was, was composed of people who shared a common life in the village. But at a time when the village or suburbia is the place from which one commutes to his place of work, the village congregation loses its secular reality. There is today everywhere an attempt to find new forms of congregational unity. When a congregation such as gathers at the City Temple in London or Riverside Church in New York seeks to become a unit of common life, this search takes the form of weekday church activities. Such a search is futile—not that weekday church activities may not be a success, but that they constitute marginal interests in the lives of those who take part in them.

Units of common life can be formed by those engaged in the same occupation, those studying or teaching in the same university, those taking part in some aspect of the civil rights movement, those belonging to the same trade union or employers' federation, and so on. It is not yet clear how to reconcile the concept of the family as the unit of the congregation and the concept of the congregation as determined by the unities of common life. The point, however, is clear: The secular world provides the unities for church structures.

On the next level comes the unity provided by a nation and, within that nation, of language or race groups. Indeed, in the United States, the existence of some black churches may not at all be a bad thing, provided no church is legislated white or black. Here again, a way must be found to express the unity of the nation without denying the identity of differences within it. And then, on the world level, there is the need to give expression to world unity without denying the unities of the nations.

When the COSMOS consultations were going on and my view was canvassed, I expressed my basic position in these words: "I cannot under any circumstances subscribe to the concept of a World Methodist Church. I am prepared to discuss any plan which recognizes Methodist churches in the plural." It seems to me that we cannot start with a World Methodist Church which then finds national and local forms. We have to find appropriate forms for providing a common life for local churches, first at the local level, then at the national level, and then at the world level.

Thus, I would say that the World Methodist Council is a legitimate expression of Methodist identity on the world level. But should an attempt be made to give the World Methodist Council a presence at the regional or national levels, such an attempt would be illegitimate. What is needed on the regional or national levels is for Methodist denominations to find effective participation there as denominations or churches (in the plural) in the life and witness of the Christian community as a whole. I can grant theoretically the possibility of Asian Methodists forming an Asian Methodist Council, if they want such a council. (They certainly do not want it.) But, in that case, and if similar action is taken in other regions, the World Methodist Council would be composed of regional Methodist councils. The point I am making is that the structure must grow from the roots upward. To reverse the process is wrong and would create confusion.

It is often contended that a global unity is what we want, and that the smaller loyalties are necessarily centrifugal. What is not seen is that global unities are necessarily power structures maintained by a balance of power within them. A Methodist global unity will inevitably be dominated by the more powerful Methodist bodies. What we need is not a structure from up going down, but a growth from down going up.

Let me now refer to a detail which, however, is of major importance. If the Methodist people are one people, must not a way be found of achieving Methodist unity at least in every country? I do not know enough to discuss this question as it appears on the American scene, but I certainly can say that the presence of more than one Methodist denomination in the same country in Asia is a tragic anomaly. Specifically, Methodist denominations that stem from America and Methodist denominations that stem from Britain must come together in the countries of Asia without continuing their separate existence. The situation becomes comic when the various Methodist denominations in America project themselves on the African scene. African Christian leaders know the financial advantage of this development, but they are becoming more and more sensitive to the false image of the church which this divisiveness creates in their countries. Of course, at the base of this kind of problem lies the simple fact that money is available in the United States of America for churches to go it alone, promoting policies which are theologically indefensible and which are not even allowed to be brought for decision to a common forum.

Can we accept as strategy, immediately and urgently, the ideal of only one Methodist denomination in each country, a system of covenanted relationships between Methodist denominations to preserve historic ties and facilitate mutual support, and a World Methodist Council or a Methodist Conference of Churches which is in no sense ecclesial in character?

2. At the Local Level

What of the involvement of Methodist churches with other churches at the local level? During the last forty years, church union discussions have been concerned largely with creating united churches in a country or in a region. Today there is emerging a parallel discussion on how, in spite of denominational differences, the Christian community in a locality can find and live a common life. This is a discussion that goes very much beyond the earlier discussion concerning interdenominational work. As a result of the new experiments which are being made with respect to congregational structure, denominationalism at the local level is proving to be increasingly irrelevant. A simple example would be the Christians in a university. To divide them into denominational congregations would be manifestly absurd. This irrelevance is further heightened by the fact that there is a new mood of conviction concerning the place of sacraments and the ordained ministry in the life of the church.

During the negotiations for church union in Ceylon, whenever I went to England, I would discuss the problems we were facing in the course of our negotiations with some of the leading thinkers on this subject in the various denominations there. On the Anglican side, the person to whom I went again and again for advice and counsel was Dr. Rawlinson, Bishop of Derby. On my last visit with him, he said something to me which I have never forgotten, and which has in the last years proved to be theologically prophetic. He said, "There are two dominical sacraments—Holy Baptism and Holy Communion. All churches agree that the former can be administered by laymen. Why then is it necessary to hold that the latter can be celebrated only by ordained ministers?"

The discussion today is increasingly centering on two is-sues. Is ordination a sacrament? Does it confer "character"? Or, must the church turn to a recognition of various forms of ministry in the church and by the church, for all of which provision must be made in some form of ordering? What is the correspondence between "ordination" and the "charis-mata"? It can be seen that in the context of this kind of ques-tioning, any argument which seeks comparison, for instance between Methodist bishops and Anglican or Lutheran bishops, is quite beside the point. The question simply becomes what kinds of ministry does this church need at this time and with what gifts for its ministry has God endowed it? In the face of such a question, the traditional powers of the Methodist episcopate are as unimportant as the historicity of any other form of episcopacy.

As for the other issue, let me put it in this way. During the last thirty years, in all my work in student and youth Christian organizations, one of the burning questions in any planning committee was that of intercommunion. Today there is a lull in this debate, an increasing tendency just not to bother about it. If there are those who want separate and separated Communion services, let them. If there are those who want a service of intercommunion, let them if they can arrange it. Holy Communion is being relegated to the area of personal religion only, and is being looked upon as having no significance as an issue in a time when the social and public implications of the faith are the main concern.

Thus, at the local level there is growing up what some have called the practice of "secular ecumenism," a practice which includes intercommunion as a matter of personal decision by the communicant, without reference to church rule or discipline. This is beginning to be true even of Roman Catholics. To revert to what I said at the very beginning, the consuming concern of ecumenism is that the church should become visible in the world. The result is that the starting point of discussion is the world and not the churches. It would be a tragedy if the movement which we have designated by the term "secular ecumenism" should overtake the ecumenical movement as we know it. For, if that should happen, there is the possibility that continuity in the life of the church would be lost. The heritage of the past should not just be dissipated; it must provide the resources for contemporary obedience. It must become wealth to be spent rather than remain riches to be stored. The trouble is that denominations are so anxious about their riches that they put them into fixed deposit. The interest earned is small. In the meanwhile the capital remains useless.

What is important is to recognize that ecclesial ecumenism and secular ecumenism together constitute the dynamic of the ecumenical enterprise; so that, to revert to the illustration already referred to, the issue of intercommunion must not be dealt with in purely ecclesiastical terms.

3. Church Union Negotiations

It has seemed to me that only against the background of the issues we have considered so far does a discussion of specific questions raised in church union negotiations make sense. To a consideration of these in some detail we must now turn. Here I would restrict myself to the negotiations in Ceylon for a united body to be called the Church of

Lanka. It is easier to be specific this way. Besides, most of the issues in church union negotiations are the same everywhere.

The more I have studied the Bible, the more I have been convinced that those who belong to Jesus Christ and carry his name are not only one family, but have to live as members of one family. Those who do not as yet believe in Jesus Christ have to be challenged by the gospel which is proclaimed as well as by those who proclaim it. When our Lord prayed that his people may be one, the reason he gave was that the world may believe in the mission of the Son. The unity of the church is a sign of the mission of Jesus Christ. It is the firstfruits of his work of reconciliation in the world.

My own work in the church, both in Ceylon and abroad, has convinced me that theological conviction is so much shaped by and bound up with nontheological history that the only safe course to follow, in order to be obedient, is to be willing to belong with one's fellow Christians in increasingly uniting churches except where subscription is demanded to theological, liturgical, or ethical positions which are a burden to one's conscience. That I do not personally like a particular view or rule or practice is irrelevant. My likes and dislikes are immaterial.

Common sense tells me that in seeking church union we should be willing to take the next step—that is, the next positive step—even though by that step the whole problem of church union as such is not solved. In Ceylon, for instance, all the churches are not together seeking church union; but for me it would be disobedience to use this fact as a reason for not agreeing to belong with those who are willing to belong with me in one church.

In the *Scheme of Church Union* in Ceylon, there are many provisions which I personally would have liked to have been made differently, but there is nothing in the *Scheme* which is a burden on my conscience. Let me here deal specifically with three of the issues which are constantly in debate.

The Ministry: Since New Testament times there have been in the order of the church three particular functions—the diaconal, the presbyteral, and the episcopal. All three belong together in the ministry of the church and are structural to the nature of the church. It is a misunderstanding when any of these functions is spoken of as a "form of government." The ordained ministry shares with the laity in the government of the church, but the ministerial office is not an office of government.

Different church polities have located these three functions differently within the structure of the church. But in none of these polities is any one of the three absent. I find no theological reason why one particular form of location should be preferred to another, even though the historical differences between them may commend one form rather than another in a particular situation. This is why, in the Ceylon *Scheme*, there are both the acceptance of the historic episcopate and the provisions that no particular doctrine of the threefold ordering of the ministry will be demanded, and that the fact that other churches do not follow the rule of episcopal ordination will not preclude the Church of Lanka from holding relations of communion and fellowship with them.

The Lord's Supper: There is no gainsaying that in the New Testament the Lord's Supper is set within the context of a common family life. When the church is divided, a double problem is posed. On the one hand, the practice of intercommunion between divided churches is a recognition of the fact that, in spite of our division, we are one people. On the other hand, limitations on the practice of intercommunion are a recognition of the fact that the church is indeed divided. The simple practice of intercommunion does violence to the integrity of the church in which faith, order, and sacrament belong together in an indivisible whole. And yet, where the practice is denied, violence is done to the *given-ness* of the church, which *given-ness* we cannot undo, not even by our divisions. There is no logical way out of this anomalous situation.

What we are seeking to do in Ceylon is to provide for a period before organic union takes place when there would be the practice of intercommunion between the churches. The sacrament of Holy Communion is a sacrament of reconciling grace.

The Sacrament of Baptism: The Baptist emphasis, and also the emphasis of all Congregational churches, is on the church as a gathered community. This emphasis has meant, in the Baptist tradition, the putting of the sacrament of baptism at a particular place in the ordering of the church's life. While not denying the nature of the Christian church as a gathered community, there are those who would emphasize equally the nature of the church as a historic community. These persons would locate baptism normally at another point in the ordering of the church's life. In the Ceylon *Scheme of Church Union*, the key provision on this question is to set out what is termed "the full Service of Initiation of Believers." Baptism is a part of that service. It allows a person to receive baptism as either an infant or a believer. The act of sponsored infant baptism is made dependent on and is

142

derived from the service. Parents of a child will decide whether sponsored baptism is to be administered to him, or whether he will be dedicated in infancy and baptized later as a believer. It is not a vain hope that, within the Church of Lanka, the increasing habit will be to have children dedicated in infancy, so that as believers later they may come to the full Service of Initiation.[2]

I have chosen the above three issues, not only because they are important, but because they demonstrate the impossibility of "tidy solutions" to our theological problems. How can we have tidy solutions when we have to reckon not only with the history of past controversies, but also with our predicament that in theological matters "we see in a mirror dimly"? To assert that one is right and that the other is wrong, and to do this unequivocally, is to forget our limitations not only as human beings but as sinners.

Besides, there is the simple fact that we do not know how to say theologically that the church is divided. Thus, it seems an obvious thing to us Methodists to say that the divided churches are equally churches; yet, if that is so, it is not obvious how the church is divided. Did the church break up into equal pieces? It seems that all that one can say with confidence is that God is equally gracious with us all.

In all such questions, does not our real difficulty lie where we confront the mystery of God's grace? On the one hand, we must affirm the sovereignty of that grace; while, on the other hand, we must accept also that grace is not unconditional. God, in his graciousness, makes demands of obedience. The Hindu protests that because grace is sovereign, the

[2] *Ceylon, North India, Pakistan: A Study in Ecumenical Decision*, Stephen F. Bayne, Jr., ed. (London: SPCK, 1960), pp. 26-27.

demand for faith in Jesus Christ is an unacceptable demand. It insists, the Hindu contends, on a restricting particularity. Those who belong to the Society of Friends will not celebrate the sacraments, for to them that is an attempt to channel God's grace. The Brethren will not accept that there is any special grace in ordination, while those who belong to non-episcopal churches will not accept that God's grace is channeled in any way through the episcopacy. It is obvious that the way to meet these protests is not to validate them all.

Particularity does characterize God's ways of grace with men, and yet every particular for which claims are made has to meet its protest in the name of him in whom there is no partiality. What we must learn to do is to take our stand on that boundary where the particular meets with its protest, and there find not an answer to our questions, for there is no final answer, but find instead the grace to meet the demands of grace.

This leads me to make two specific points, both of which illustrate the difficulty, if not the impossibility, of what I have called "tidy solutions."

In church union discussions a common source of confusion is the different perspectives from which the argument is conducted. There are those for whom the primary question is, "Is this necessary for salvation?" There are others who ask, "Is this part of the given structure of the church?" There are still others who ask, "Since the church has not only to be the church but has also to be a church that is visibly one, what are the marks of this visibility?"

The discussion of no issue stays within any one of these perspectives, with the result that an answer given to a question can be right in terms of one perspective and yet be open to serious misunderstanding in terms of another. It is not only impossible to get everybody to accept a particular perspective as the perspective from which the discussion must be conducted, but it is also impossible to keep the discussion within one perspective. There is, therefore, a necessary confusion in the discussion.

A good example of this confusion is the way in which a discussion about Holy Communion gets involved in a discussion about ordination. The two are related, and yet to the question of how they are related there can be many answers.

Another source of confusion is that while the churches are divided, each one has its own self-understanding, and articulates that self-understanding both positively and negatively. In the case of the Baptist church, for instance, there are the positive teaching on believers' baptism and the negative teaching on paedobaptism. Similar instances can be given for the other churches. When union takes place between these churches, the problem will arise of how to move away from a past characterized by division into a future characterized by unity.

The Ceylon plan of union makes one significant contribution toward resolving this difficulty. It says, "In laying down laws and principles for the life of the Church of Lanka, the uniting Churches do not seek thereby to express a judgment upon the teaching or practice of the uniting Churches hitherto." [3] (The "teaching or practice" is whether positive or negative.) It is important that the churches accept this position, so that they do not expect solutions to the problems between them as a preparation and prerequisite for union. It

[3] *Ibid.*, p. 23.

is in union that they will find many of the answers that elude them now.

The essential thing is to realize that church union is not primarily an administrative act. It is an acceptance of healing and wholeness from God himself. Not only does a church go to God as it is, but it allows the other churches to do the same. The united church must in God's mercy be a *new creation.*

There are those who think that the constitution of a united church should be hammered out in detail before union. For some of them, dissent from a provision in a scheme of union as to how bishops should be paid is sufficient reason for voting against the scheme. I have a feeling that when the churches in Ceylon which are now in union negotiations have united, they will find that many constitutional provisions, even in the present *Scheme,* will need thorough revision. But that is as it should be. What is so grievous is that so many who bear the name of Christ are so distrustful of their brethren that they are not prepared to take any risks whatsoever with them. In the last analysis, a vote for church union is a vote to trust those who belong with us in the household of faith.

But it is objected by some that while they are for union, it is a particular scheme which they do not like. All I can say is that, in the discussion in Ceylon, I have not yet heard a single one of these people say that some particular provision of the *Scheme* is a burden on his conscience. Rather, they claim that it is a burden on their logic, their wisdom, or their theology. I cannot personally bring myself to reject something because it does not square with my logic or theology, or because I think it unwise. I am prepared to argue, and then fall in line once the decision is made. To follow any other course would be spiritually dangerous.

I must add a personal word here. I have been a member of the Negotiating Committee in Ceylon since its very beginning in 1945 and can testify to the fact how, again and again, God by the grace of the Holy Spirit kept us moving, often in spite of ourselves and always beyond our expectation. It is this experience which gives us hope and sustains the assurance that he will see us through. He will not leave unfinished what he has begun.

There is another matter to which I must refer. There are those who are so disillusioned with the institutional church and who so want what has now come to be called in many circles "religionless Christianity" that they have no patience whatever with problems of church union as such. We are in a curious situation. Those who have a tendency to judge everything in the sphere of religion in terms of what is necessary for salvation, or in terms of what is ordered in the New Testament, find the church union scheme dealing with many things which seem to them quite unimportant and unnecessary. Others whose overriding concern is the gospel for the world think that the quest for church union is a waste of time. They would rather work for a secular revolution in the church as a direct objective. Personally, I have great sympathy for these points of view. But I find myself constantly asking whether God's way with us in Ceylon may not be by a detour. May it not be that we shall find both the grace that saves and the truth that revolutionizes by seeking to obey this concrete and specific demand to unite—which is fundamentally the demand to love? It is very rare that the treasure we seek is found by some direct method. "He who went to plow found a treasure" (cf. Matt. 13:44)

Let me confess that in my own attitude toward church union I have been driven just as much by fear as by faith. I am constantly haunted by the fact that when the Messiah actually came, he came in such a form that those who had prayed for him rejected him. All of us in our churches have prayed that God will guide the church in Ceylon into new ways of obedience and victory. That the challenge to union is part of God's answer to our prayers I find it difficult to disbelieve—primarily because it is coming as such a demanding challenge, as something with implications many of which we do not relish. Dr. George McLeod, in his John Knox lecture, says that as far as he has read church history he cannot recall a single instance in which the church obeyed its Lord except under the pressure of the world.[4] This is a sobering thought. It is impossible to predict how, in our various countries and situations, we shall feel the pressures of the world. Generalizations will be false. But this much is true: We must expect a congruence between the ways of God in the world and the ways of God with his church. The Head of the church is also Lord of the world.

4. Conclusion

I was asked to deal with the subject given to me from an Asian point of view. I have not attempted to do this by speaking of Asia as such or the challenges we face there today as Christians. These have been spoken about many times, and the point has been made again and again that in a

[4] *John Knox and Today* (Geneva: John Knox Association, 1959).

148

world of competing religions, rising secularism, hunger, and underdevelopment, the church has to prove its mission by what it itself is. What I have attempted to do, rather, is to speak as a person from Asia, living there and working from there. I have also attempted to speak as a member of the Methodist family. I can be frank with my fellow Methodists in a way in which non-Methodists cannot be.

I would end where I began, and that is with a plea that we Methodists, along with our fellow Christians, move from our established positions to go on that pilgrimage to which we are bidden, journeying to the land of our inheritance, even though we go out not knowing where to go (Heb. 11:8).

vii
methodism and ecumenism in the united states

Methodism is one of the most American of the denominational expressions of Christianity. This judgment, first expressed by Philip Schaff a century ago, has been recently repeated and emphasized by Jaroslav Pelikan.[1] To the extent that this historical and social judgment is true, American ecumenism must take the various forms of Methodism seriously, and to that extent The United Methodist Church must shape its ecumenical stance with a high sense of responsibility. When Schaff and Pelikan make their judgments they are not only offering a partial interpretation of American church history, but they are implying something as well about the religious faith, order, and organization of denominational life. To be American does not mean to be right ecumenically or morally, but to be American involves the recognition of certain factors in church and national life that tend to shape religious movements and institutions, the forms of theology, ecclesiastical organizations, and social teaching and action.

A hundred years ago Methodism was the largest denominational grouping in the nation. Today this is no longer true; on the contrary, the pluralistic character of American life is evident, with Roman Catholics constituting the largest single church. Despite the pluralism of belief and unbelief in the United States and the large influx of Roman Catholics, Jews, and persons from countries where Orthodoxy predominates, all religious bodies have undergone a process of Amer-

[1] Jaroslav J. Pelikan, "Methodism's Contribution to America," in *The History of American Methodism*, E. S. Bucke, ed. (Nashville: Abingdon Press, 1964), III, 596-608.

icanization. Through many forces America has influenced the religious life of disparate groups such as Irish, Italian, and Polish Catholics, Eastern European and German Jews, and Greek, Armenian, and Russian Orthodox. They have not grown up with the nation in quite the same way as have the Methodists, but they have been influenced by that Protestant style which Methodists developed in their adaptation to the forces that shaped the nineteenth and early twentieth centuries. The adaptation, adjustment, and accommodation made by many Protestant and non-Protestant bodies to American culture have the imprint of that form of evangelical Protestantism which Methodism contributed to frontier life and to rural and urban settings in almost two centuries of activity. Pelikan has aptly observed that "Methodism succeeded so well in shaping the typically American understanding of religion that the Americanization of other churches, notably of those churches whose origins lay on the European Continent, entailed the adoption of Methodist practices and 'new measures.' " [2]

The pervasive influence of Americanized Methodism on the theology and church life of the United States, as well as its past influence on the culture and morals of the nation, may mean that Methodism has already made its greatest contribution to ecumenism in this country. In saying this I am not making exclusive Methodist claims, nor am I putting all the evidence on the positive side. The subsequent discussion will frankly disavow any such temptation. I am saying that Methodism is very much an American phenomenon and that it had great influence in shaping church life and thought in a period when other religious bodies from Europe,

[2] *Ibid.*, p. 599.

whether Lutheran or Roman Catholic, were being trans-
muted from state churches abroad to denominations here.

Because the ecumenical movement now developing among
American denominations bears the imprint of Methodist in-
fluence, Methodists should feel at home in that movement.
Methodism does not stand over against ecumenism in the
United States, but is pervasively a part of it.

Today American Methodists are seriously attempting to
chart their ecumenical course. When Christians consider what
treasures they have to bring to the marriage feast of ecumenism, they characteristically consult their traditions in theology,
polity, and social history. This stance is a bit awkward for
Methodists to assume. It makes us far more self-conscious
than others. Our historical vocation has not been to protect
a "deposit." Because we were in practice shaped by American
political institutions and by the frontier, like the frontier we
stood loose to the ties of tradition, whether religious or cultural. There is plenty of treasure for Methodists to dig out
of the past, and Methodist scholars have performed a useful
service in recovering the rich resources available in the
thought of John Wesley. They have done so, however, without falling into the errors of making a new confessionalism
out of the Wesleyan heritage or of attempting to parade it
before other Christians.

If we want the treasure and *power* of Methodism brought
fully into the ecumenical pilgrimage, we must look for it
not in the eighteenth century as an imitation or recollection
of the Wesleys. That might formalize or even legalize this
evangelical treasure. We must, rather, look to where they
found the *power:* in the earlier periods of the church that
knew "scriptural holiness" firsthand and in those centuries

when renewal and reform of the nations were the order of the day. Nineteenth-century Methodists were committed to that task; they risked putting evangelical Christianity to work in a period of very rapid social change, adapting mission and institutions, task forces and lay ministry, to the receding frontier. And when the frontier was gone geographically, they turned to social frontiers as new dimensions of evangelical concern. Witness the "Social Creed"!

Methodists took a pragmatic risk and applied the gospel of God's judgment and grace to frontier conditions and to the needs of new communities. Theirs was a victory, but it was won with a heavy price of accommodation and adjustment—a price we are still paying. Through what they and others accomplished, a free evangelical Protestant establishment emerged. In it the Methodist treasure is to be found, but it is rather heavily encased. What Methodism now needs is to be saved from that success and, in responding to the last third of the twentieth century, to become as provisional in its structures as it was formerly. It needs an evangelical realism and a practical contemporary understanding that recognizes that all churches together have a common American and world mission in an age of computers, instantaneous communication, cocktail gossip hours, and city renewal.

A clue to the future progress of unity among all the churches may lie in an authentic evangelical commitment such as related the original Methodist movement to the Church of England and transcended the aridity of its institutionalism. The early Wesleyan spirit was open to all the previous centuries of Christian experience. This spirit was not indifferent to what was at once catholic, reformed, and evangelical. It did not make a new confessionalism out of its own renewal in the Holy Spirit. It recognized the need to bring the whole of life under the mandate of perfection and to have a dynamic understanding of what sanctification means when lived out in the midst of daily social existence. Recent ecumenical studies point to the central need to let the Holy Spirit once again make his home in the church and renew it. This current emphasis on the renewal of the church through the Holy Spirit has many affinities with the practical theology of the evangelical revival in that it seeks to be fully trinitarian—recognizing the centrality of Jesus Christ in redemption and the creative power and order of God the Father.

Methodism's ecumenical stance is not anti-theological, or even anti-confessional, and surely not anti-intellectual. It should represent—and at its best does represent—renewal in the sense of integral wholeness of the gospel and all the valid treasures of the church's witness. Methodism finds dialogue with other Christian bodies congenial because its history proceeds not from intellectual controversy but from a quest for holiness, which also is a quest for wholeness.

At present The United Methodist Church's ecumenical stance is being developed and tested largely in relation to the Consultation on Church Union. The Consultation has produced a remarkable consensus on the specifically theological questions that have come before it. On basic doctrinal issues there appear to be no insuperable barriers to unity. The statement *Principles of Church Union*[3] shows that through the decades of dialogue in state, national, and world councils of churches a common mind has been emerging regarding

[3] Consultation on Church Union 1967, *Principles of Church Union* (Cincinnati, Forward Movement Publications).

154

the church's ministry and sacraments, its corporate nature, the call to solidarity in its mission, the central and integral place of worship and the Christian service of God, and the general meaning of ordination and a representative ministry.

To be sure, residual differences exist, and latent issues will become explicit in the next two years as a plan of union is defined and debate on it begins. Such debate will enliven the ecumenical movement in the United States, because the people will have to make decisions and because familiar ways of work, fellowship, and worship may be changed. There will be resistance, but there will be hope for many.

Some realistic factors that confront this quest for renewal and unity must be faced, and we shall attend to a number of them. First we must note, however, that the general theological consensus which is expressed in the *Principles* is undoubtedly even broader than that of the churches represented in COCU. In the address by Monsignor Tucci at the Uppsala Assembly of the World Council of Churches it was evident that there are no insuperable theological barriers to the membership of the Roman Catholic Church in the Council. There was also general concurrence by the delegates of the Orthodox Churches and the Roman Catholic observers in the section report on "The Holy Spirit and Catholicity." The churches in the Consultation on Church Union must take full account of all the theological implications of aggressive ecumenism in the Orthodox and Roman Catholic Churches and the common understanding of catholicity that commended itself at Uppsala.

We must keep this wider context always in mind as we consider the place and problems of Methodism in the American scene.

155

There are persistent influences in the American scene which worked for the earlier success of the churches' unity and mission but which now are dysfunctional. It is striking that what works against unity today also works against mission. This generalization will hold for other denominations as well as for Methodists. The starting points may be different because of ethnic, racial, or polity factors, but the problems are analogous.

Among these influences, the following eight are prominent: voluntarism, sermon-centered evangelism, rural parish patterns, sectionalism or regionalism, race, size and connectionalism, social control and moralism, and institutionalism.

1. Voluntarism. In a sense all American denominations are voluntary associations. There is no determination of religion by the state, no tax support, and no legal priority with parish boundaries set on a geographical basis. Congregations are gathered freely. Persons migrate from church to church according to their desires, and such migration has increased. Voluntarism has been established as a principle in church polity and has a theological sanction in the idea of religious liberty.

Voluntarism may become an ideological factor to resist effective church union. By "ideological factor" I mean the use of an idea to serve the past, to resist change, or to defend the *status quo.* A recent proposal on the United Church of Christ's structure states:

Local churches are the foundation of the United Church of Christ. They are autonomous, but are bound together by common purpose and voluntary co-operation. . . . In keeping with the church's theology and polity, the constitution of the United Church of Christ in Section 21 provides that "The autonomy of the local church is inherent and modifiable only by its own action." This autonomy exists within a tradition and practice of voluntary co-operation.[4]

In trying to develop a new national structure the denomination has to work through and wrestle with the ideological factors of local autonomy and voluntarism. When autonomy becomes an end in itself, it works to the disadvantage of the total effort of the church and becomes a bar both to denominational planning and to ecumenical expressions of ministry.

Voluntarism in Methodism contributed to its early rapid growth, but it now places an ideological restraint on the updating, renewing, and unifying of the denomination. The principle of voluntarism is expressed in the combined power of annual conferences and jurisdictions which enables them to slow down the abolition of racism and segregation by rejecting a mandatory date to change ecclesiastical structures.

2. Sermon-centered Evangelism. The nineteenth century was the era of the orator in politics and of the preacher-evangelist. Churches grew as the preacher inspired a following of laymen who were willing to support him. In the *laissez-faire* marketplace of preaching some men grew to great heights of effectiveness; others in the same communities had more modest success. Salaries and congregational size generally reflected the competition of evangelical zeal and pulpit prowess. Methodism had its share of great preachers. Bishops were expected to be first of all outstanding evangelistic or prophetic preachers. When famous lectureships in preaching were established in theological seminaries, Methodists

[4] "Tentative Report of the Committee on Structure, United Church of Christ."

were chosen quite frequently because of their reputations in the field.

But there is a dark and subtle side to the preaching era of American denominations. The voluntary idea combined with financial support by the laity to tempt church leaders to compromise the gospel by adapting it to the tastes of regions and classes. Individualism in the American churches was symbolic—reflecting both the theological perspective of the preacher and the message that laymen were willing to pay for. It has been said often that Calvinism had success in America only as it transformed itself into "an operational Arminianism." [5] It must be added that evangelistic preaching, under the subtle influences of voluntary support and the dangers of migrating congregations, too often developed an "operational gospel" which contributed to the rise later of "culture religion."

Some of the crasser forms of pulpiteer-dominated congregational life have been mitigated in Methodism by the combined forces of itinerancy and connectionalism. But there can be no doubt that it established some patterns of localism in which pastors have become very possessive and protective of the time and talents of laymen and do not encourage them greatly in ecumenical endeavors. We are slowly working out of the idea of the local church as a preaching station into a more wholistic idea. Today the preacher cannot carry the load alone—and he never could. Ecumenism is furthered as informed laymen are organized to fulfill the ministry of the congregation in the world. They are motivated to unity as they seek to change society.

[5] *The Shaping of American Religion,* James W. Smith and A. Leland Jamison, eds. (Princeton: Princeton University Press, 1961), p. 362.

3. Rural Methodism. At one time the glory of Methodism was its town and country churches. To be relevant to the frontier meant to be rural. The stamp of rural community life has deeply shaped the character of the Methodist circuit, the idea of the parish, and the expectations and goals of ministry. Today's civilization is being determined by the city, yet most Protestant local churches are still rural. It is very difficult to unite rural churches within a denomination and even more difficult to do so across denominational boundaries. In assessing Methodism's ecumenical obligation, role, and prospects, the factors of the rural establishment are a major influence. People cling to rural and local loyalties with great tenacity. Great courage at the denominational top will be required to effect the cooperation and union of competing small town and rural churches across denominational barriers. Today in many of these places energies go into bare institutional subsistence; educational standards for the ministry are depressed; and defensive attitudes resist ecumenical ventures. Half the nation's poor are rural. They must not be abandoned.

The ecumenical dilemmas of the countryside follow the shift of population from farm to city. Particularly today the great majority of immigrants to the city are the rural poor. They are naturally seeking the securities they counted on in their place of origin. Yet the rural church in the city hardly meets their new problems. Nevertheless, we must understand the need of such persons for the quality of community that was provided in the rural-type church. They look for the church to do for them what a displaced church type simply cannot do, and in their expectations they do not enhance the ecumenical situation.

Several of our large denominations are neither unified nor renewed because they have not found a common strategy for the rural church in its natural setting or for the rural church as a transitional institution in the urban setting.

Today the city is dominant, and it calls for an integrated metropolitan strategy. Its ways are not the ways of the frontier or the family farm or the small town. Its values reflect everybody's individual goals. Its values also reflect the interests of giant corporations, powerful trade unions, big government, and other impersonal interests. The city makes possible the glory of the arts and the universities, and it also sorts out people with cruel impersonality into dwellers of plush highrise apartment houses and barrios and ghettos. The arts, the universities, the affluent chrome and plastic cliffs, and the barrios are all baffling areas for the ministry of a traditional rural-type parish church to penetrate. Holding companies and financial corporations are cold beasts of the urban jungle whose law and order no longer conceal the violence that erupts in urban riots. Urbanization—particularly in megalopolitan areas—has become the chattel of predatory commercial interests, of crime syndicates, of corrupted politicians, of exploiters of race prejudice and poverty, of the returned soldiery, and of vulgar mass communications media. These forces turn a deaf, computerized ear to the appeals and protests of churches that have no effective programming. They are able to ignore the divided and naïve churches because their models of the pulpit voice of the mid-nineteenth century and self-centered community parish are unsuited to deal with the power structures of the final third of the twentieth century. They are able to do so also because the voluntarism of the churches is so often wedded to the values of the *status quo*. The church is often weakest where the crises are deepest, because the social system as a whole needs structural reforming in its priorities and the churches are accommodated to the classes that resist needed social change.

4. *Regionalism*. The Americanization of churches has involved regionalism or sectionalism. Though the Civil War resolved the question of the federal unity of the national state, it did not overcome the sectional dismemberment of Methodism. Regionalism involved not only the question of racial division according to both class and caste, but it also involved important issues concerning the role and authority of bishops and of the General Conference. By the 1939 unification of the Methodist Episcopal Church, the Methodist Episcopal Church, South, and the Methodist Protestant Church, the jurisdictional structure was made a safeguard for regional interests, especially in the South. The jurisdictional structure—minus the segregated Central Jurisdiction— persists in The United Methodist Church and sometimes is a source of a demonic type of voluntarism. Since 1939 episcopacy has become more provincial, and theological education has tended to drift into regional support patterns and therefore into regional recruitment patterns. The modest growth of appreciation for the idea that all the seminaries are theological centers for the whole denomination has won out since unification despite the jurisdictional organization. The nationwide support plan adopted by the 1968 General Conference should assist in reducing regionalism in theological education in the future.

Regionalism is a major problem for the future of ecumenical relations, because some denominations, with their distinctive ethos and polities, are highly concentrated in certain

161

states. Only a strong national organization will be able to transcend the forces inherent in ecclesiastical ideologies marked by a combination of voluntarism, autonomy, and localism. Yet regional organization may be necessary when unification embraces such large numbers (about twenty-five million) as are in the member denominations of the Consultation on Church Union. In the longer future, unification with the regionally concentrated Lutherans and the urban-minded Roman Catholics will be major challenges. Lutherans alone have nine million adherents.

The problems of a regional mentality as reflected in a jurisdictional system are failure to hear or heed the mind of the whole church and failure to effect in every place what the will of the whole church is. It was this problem which the great practical ecumenist, Bishop G. Bromley Oxnam, attacked in 1956 in an address to the Northeastern Jurisdiction. He pointed out that the jurisdictional Colleges of Bishops

have the tendency to become caucuses in which the mind of a region is made up before the Council of Bishops meets, which means that decision is reached before the case of the whole church is heard. These meetings are close to the pressures of the local scene. There is the danger of responding too quickly to sectional prejudice. . . . Men who think in diocesan terms seldom think in world terms.[6]

What is a tendency in a regional college of bishops is even more a difficulty for church leaders who seldom come in contact with those from outside the region. Since ecumenism

[6] *Journal of the Fifth Northeastern Jurisdictional Conference of The Methodist Church* (1956), pp. 258, 263.

is a concern for the church as a whole, regional self-absorption tends to give it a low priority.

5. *Racial Factors.* The forces which have been thus far briefly defined and analyzed are intensified by white racism and its attendant prejudice and segregation. With the elimination of the Central Jurisdiction, integration in The United Methodist Church is accelerating. Approximately 350,000 Negroes are involved. In addition, the three major independent bodies of Negro Methodists total about 11,400 congregations with a combined membership of 2,340,000 members. Each of these is a member of the National Council of Churches and of the World Council of Churches. They have been members for a long while, yet not much has happened. Such memberships show the limitations of mere cooperative ecumenism. The African Methodist Episcopal Church has thirteen episcopal districts in the United States, the A.M.E. Zion Church has twelve, and the Christian Methodist Episcopal Church has nine. It is noteworthy that these denominations are heavily rural and regional. Organizational unification would present many problems mostly of a nontheological character, i.e. economic, educational, and strategic. They are compounded by the rapidly changing aspects of the racial and urban revolution and by the challenges of black leadership and black poverty.

Nowhere is the changing role of the ministry in American society more evident than in the black denominations, particularly in the Methodist and Baptist bodies. The United States census in 1910 noted 17,495 Negro clergymen; they comprised 14.8 percent of all Negro professional workers. By 1930 the number increased to 25,034, or 16.8 percent of such workers. Clergymen constituted the second largest group among Negro professional workers and enjoyed a complete monopoly behind the caste wall. It was the only profession in which Negroes had more representatives than the general population. No doubt this phenomenon was related to the then strict caste situation, to the nature and function of Negro church life, much of it rural, and to the relative ease with which one could be educated for the ministry and thus attain the status of a professional. Important changes have occurred in all three dimensions of black churchmanship, but these changes have not been great enough to correct a scandalous division in the church of Christ. Myrdal said in 1944 that the Negro church was losing out among the young people, mostly because the Negro preacher had lagged behind the rest of the Negro community and particularly behind other professionals in acquiring a better education.[7] A mission to Negro youth today, therefore, requires special attention to education, jobs, and community leadership among black people.

As predominantly white and predominantly Negro churches confront each other, they present the dilemmas of complementary accommodation to segregation. On the one hand, white Methodism's accommodation to slavery is indicated by the fact that Methodists owned no less than 200,000 slaves. White racism in the denomination was the result.[8] On the other hand, black Methodism accommodated with docility to the same situation. Today we see a militancy of black Methodists which is much needed if unification is to take place. The demand for restructuring the church at local, annual

---

[7] Gunnar Myrdal, *An American Dilemma* (New York: Harper and Row, 1944), pp. 872-78.

[8] A. C. Cole, *The Irrepressible Conflict, 1850-1865* (New York: Macmillan, 1934), p. 258.

conference, jurisdictional, and General Conference levels is essential if creative power is to go to work for mission. It is now evident that the restructuring of society and the restructuring of the church must go together.

The question is sometimes asked whether The United Methodist Church should first pursue union with the A.M.E., A.M.E. Zion, and C.M.E. Churches and then turn to the other churches in COCU, or whether the larger union should take precedence and union with the predominantly Negro bodies be consummated within that framework. These questions are especially relevant when we consider that a Plan of Union is now being drafted in COCU. Several considerations argue in favor of a vigorous pursuit of a general Methodist union. First, such a union has the general endorsement of Negro Methodists (including Black Methodists for Church Renewal) who have a great stake in the matter. Secondly, if the will is present, the problems of education, economics, and polity can be more speedily attended to in such similar organizations than in more complex unions. Thirdly, the form of church union appropriate to COCU may not be full organic or organizational union, but such a form of union is the only one with integrity among Methodist bodies. Any union plan in COCU must go beyond mere cooperation. It must embody a reconciliation of ministries and a unification of membership, but its organizational pattern may be a federation, a pluralistic organism, or a highly unified structure. There are many possibilities. Yet, among Methodists the fullest expression of unity is required. Anything less would be tainted by some degree of segregation. One of the most urgent next steps in ecumenism must therefore be the unification and structural integration of these four bodies.

Significantly, the 1968 General Conference mandated the Commission on Ecumenical Affairs to explore union with the three Negro churches.

Because of the size and social function of Baptist bodies, special note must be taken, though briefly, of their relation to the Methodist stance. Baptists comprise almost 24,000,000 members and represent 12.2 percent of the national population, thus exceeding all Methodist bodies by almost ten million. Baptists constitute 18.9 percent of American religious membership. There have been no major Baptist mergers in the last thirty years. The Baptist family that accounts for this notable size is the Southern Baptist Convention, comprising almost half the total number. It is still predominantly "Southern" in outlook and geographical location and orientation, though it has expanded beyond the boundaries of the region. The aggressive strength of Southern Baptists in states and counties where Methodists are seeking to implement racial integration constitutes a reactionary restraint and a refuge for those who believe that The United Methodist Church is going too fast in race relations. Local autonomy, plus voluntarism, plus regionalism, plus white racism equal reactionary nonecumenism.

Historically the Baptist tradition has had a strong attraction for Negroes, but this is ironical since there is little integration within the several divisions of the Baptist family. Perhaps 63 percent of all Negro church members are Baptist, comprising 7 2/3 millions as compared with 2 3/4 millions of Methodists. It is significant that the large Negro Baptist conventions belong to the World Council of Churches and the Southern Baptists do not; this contrast has great implications for the mandate that within Methodism the challenge of union and integration be promptly met.

Methodists have their own family homework to do, but their local homework in the Southern areas is made even more difficult by the white racism of competing churches which are willing to put religious sanctions behind the Southern establishment and which aggressively attack the ecumenical efforts of the National Council of Churches.

6. *Size and Connectionalism.* The success of Methodism is often argued in terms of its size ("we must be right because we are so big") and accounted for in terms of its connectional system. At least one leader has argued that what holds Methodism together is its polity. Yet, as we have noted, the Lutheran family is quite large, the Baptist family is much larger, and the Roman Catholic Church is very much larger than Methodism. Their polities are dissimilar, though all have become quite Americanized in the sense in which we used that term in the beginning of this discussion. Size cannot be a criterion of polity preference.

Connectionalism is one of the treasures which many Methodists wish to bring into future church unions. It may, in fact, be an ideological factor comparable to autonomy and voluntarism in other denominations. On the other hand, it may very well be a practical clue to the kind of organization which is indispensable for effective church life in an urban-industrial civilization. Its usefulness in discussion will be enhanced if it is not put on the level of the principles of union already accepted by the Consultation on Church Union.

Speaking critically, Methodists' twofold structural emphases on connectionalism and itinerancy serve an ideological purpose which may resist reform in polity and practical organization. These ideas may be expressed in the phrase "every church a minister, and every minister a charge." Important theological assumptions lie behind connectionalism and itinerancy, and these assumptions may be consistent with modifications in church order and organization. One may argue as follows:

Our commitment to the connectional and itinerant emphases is focused in the interdependency of membership in the whole people of God and the fundamental unity in the itinerant ministry which is deeper than just an *esprit de corps*. . . . Our commitment might be stated to believe the local congregations are the Church of Christ, *in* themselves but not *by* themselves. This puts Methodism somewhere in between a polity of radical congregational authority and a polity of centralized authority.[9]

The functional agent of connectionalism and itinerancy is the office of bishop. There occasionally is a strong ideological element in Methodist insistence on the appointive powers of the bishop. Another such factor is sometimes the corporate or connectional ownership of church property. Much can be said for all these aspects of Methodist structure as long as their provisional character is recognized and the church is open to internal reform. A recent document circulated in the Commission on Ecumenical Affairs says rightly: "It was a general evangelical and a specific Wesleyan understanding that *any* church was provisional on behalf of the people of God. Our structures are made by men and sanctified by habit!" [10]

As we move more fully and deeply into church union, we

---

[9] Document presented to the General Commission on Ecumenical Affairs of The Methodist Church, January 3, 1968.
[10] *Ibid.*

168

must design the connectional structure of the united church in such a way as to effect its planned mission in a complex, urbanized civilization. The role of bishops has changed in the past thirty years and must be adapted further in the ecumenical era of the future. Bishops are more and more judged by their administrative skills, although this is not the basis on which they have always been elected. A large part of their time is spent attending numerous meetings of boards and committees. In such meetings the bishop presides and is expected to offer creative leadership. In addition, he has to administer his own episcopal area, chair cabinet meetings, make appointments, deliver sermons, and dedicate buildings. Power which formerly was highly concentrated in his office is now increasingly shared by other centers of power. Power to appoint is shared with the district superintendent, the local church, and the pastor; programs are qualified and emphases determined by a quadrennial program; general planning and overall denominational administration are shared with councils of secretaries and program councils. Such tasks will not diminish in a united church.

What should be the shape of the episcopal office in the new church to emerge from COCU? Should it not be largely determined by the being and mission of the church in accordance with the shape of the society of the last decades of the twentieth century? Is the parish within the Episcopal diocese the model that emerges from today's urban realities? I suggest that we take seriously some of the confirmed scientific models of urban planners with respect to the size of the planning unit. Planning must be national, regional and metropolitan. Within a metropolitan area the mission of the church will take many forms, some residential and some functional. Some will be relatively fixed, and some will be relatively mobile. A bishop confined within a large metropolitan area to a typical diocesan territory may well be an ecclesiastical relic. He may have continuity with his episcopal forebears, but he has little with the present order of secular reality.

The New Delhi Assembly of the World Council of Churches emphasized the need to manifest the unity of all Christians in each place. At the Uppsala Assembly this emphasis was enlarged to include a fresh understanding of "the unity of all Christians in all places." Uppsala added: "This calls the churches in all places to realize that they belong together and are called to act together. In a time when human interdependence is so evident, it is the more imperative to make visible the bonds which unite Christians in universal fellowship." [11]

It is quite evident now that no existing order of bishops or of episcopal surrogates is able to symbolize the catholicity and continuity of the church, much less to effect a recomposition of the divided churches. Unity and renewal are principally forwarded by various types of councils. When we are debating about bishops and the continuity and connectionalism of the churches, we are not entitled to overlook the fact that councils composed of bishops, nonbishops, and laymen are doing what no bishop or group of bishops can do. We are moving rapidly toward a form of the church that calls for a wholeness derived from many offices, functions, and new forms of ministry—clerical and lay. We are moving toward a form of the church in which the church and the secular

[11] *Uppsala Report*, p. 17.

order cooperate to serve what is personally and socially human.

7. *Social Control and Moralism.* To be indifferent to injustice and to the needs of others at home and abroad is to be as heretical as if one were to distort an article of a creed or a confessional belief. From its beginning, Methodism revolted against the heresy of formalism and unconcern for the masses. The doctrine of justification by faith required a new style of life which embraces the whole of "scriptural holiness" and is expressed in deeds to reform the nation. At the Fourth Assembly of the World Council, great emphasis was placed on the reality of the practical or ethical heresies to which Christians have surrendered. The test for Christians today is not primarily the finding of common beliefs; it is the making of a common commitment to attack the tragic evils that beset an interdependent world society.

Out of the evangelical revival of the eighteenth century a characteristic form of social control emerged among Methodists; unfortunately this mode of personal and social discipline tended to become moralistic. In her ecumenical posture today Methodism may be called to a new evangelical realism with respect to both man's inner condition and his social structures. The Wesleys rejected the "cheap grace" of formalism and stressed the "costly grace" of new birth. They rejected the "cheap prophecy" of those who make proposals for reform but do not identify in life with people who are the victims of unjust social structures and processes. A challenge to all the churches is to overcome the "cheap prophecy" of verbal analysis and high-sounding pronouncements by instilling a new will into society.

Roman Catholic leaders have occasionally looked at early

171

Methodism in England and remarked that, if it had emerged in their church, it would probably have become an order. At The United Methodist Church's 1968 General Conference, Archbishop John Joseph Carberry of St. Louis quoted with approval a remark made by the nineteenth-century Anglican scholar E. B. Pusey: "We mourn now that Wesley was not led to form an order with the Church . . . we mourn here the loss of a deep devoted fealty, of strong intellectual energy, clear-sighted faith, of ardent piety." [12]

The function of an order within the church-type body is to renew and reform while still being obedient. Its function is not separatism. To carry out the reform and to be an agent of renewal a special discipline is devised. This discipline is first and foremost a way of life for adherents of the order; thus its maturations must be intrinsic. It does not go about asking other people to pay the price of its convictions. It is neither "cheap grace" nor "cheap prophecy."

By no stretch of the imagination is Methodism, when taken as a whole, an order in the ecumenical movement, nor is it a very disciplined way of Christian living. Methodists are about as middle-class in their adjustments and as accommodated to American culture as any other Christians.

On two traditional social evils, the use of tobacco and alcoholic beverages, the formal position of the denomination is still somewhat distinctive. On questions of gambling Methodists will generally take a harder line than some other groups. But Methodists are not a truly disciplined people today. From this fact we cannot infer that delegates to the Consultation on Church Union should not press for a united church which encourages the freedom of disciplined orders within

[12] *The Daily Christian Advocate*, April 29, 1968, p. 303.

it. Indeed, justification by faith in the Christ who is Lord of the world demands both a more rigorous "No" and a more disciplined "Yes" to society than is being practiced today. Deeper than any moralism or legalism is the responsible ordering of interior life.

In these words of encouragement from Archbishop Carberry we may hear the call to renew the historically important gift of holiness in Methodist ecumenical participation:

Methodism shares with Catholicism in the interest that the ecumenical movement involves more than meshing of church machinery; that it concerns itself profoundly with the life-style of the Christian. Christians are well aware of the involvement they must have in the city of man. There are very strong parallels between the Methodist "Social Creed" and the Vatican Council's Constitution on the Church in the Modern World. These are well known and need not be restated. It is, however, our mutual desire that we impart a distinctly Christian quality to our service to the community; and this distinctive quality, I believe, is the redemptive work of the Holy Spirit.[13]

8. *Institutionalism.* In the seven major factors which we have thus far considered, we have noted both constructive adaptation and negative accommodation. On the constructive side, these factors contribute to the institutional adaptability and relevance of the church. On the negative side, they contribute to the complacency and even demonic strain in the empirical institution. In balance they help to describe the introversion of the church and its self-absorption in a divided society. The church's greatest weakness arises from its institutionalism—that organizational disease in which the means be-

[13] *Ibid.,* p. 304a.

173

comes too prominent in the ends and becomes even an end itself. Those who write the Plan of Union for the Consultation on Church Union will find that ecumenism is not a high priority for the people of God, not because they have higher priorities of mission, but because they could hardly care less. When the rank and file are not on fire with the new spirit of renewal, those who labor to unite churches are overabsorbed in making practical compromises among organizational agencies and interests.

All the denominations occasionally realize that cooperative ecumenism is not sufficient for the day in which we live. That is what we have today, and clearly it is not enough. Cooperative ecumenism points beyond itself. Its own structures perpetuate that institutionalism among the churches which creates barriers to the fuller life of the Holy Spirit.

We must pray that the Holy Spirit will give us new life and a new obedience. Though we must work for all humane causes, we need above all to confess the Holy Spirit. As the Uppsala Assembly noted, there is a ninefold gift which the Holy Spirit gives with new life in the church.

In giving this life the Holy Spirit

brings sinful men through repentance and Baptism into the universal fellowship of the forgiven;

bears witness through the Church to the truth of the Gospel, and makes it credible to men;

builds up the Church in each place through the proclamation of the Word and the celebration of the Eucharist;

stirs the conscience of the Church by the voice of prophets to keep her in the mercy and judgment of God;

maintains the Church in communion and continuity with the people of God in all ages and places;

equips the Church to accept and make use of the great variety of God's gifts bestowed upon its members for the enrichment of human life;

empowers the Church in her unity to be a ferment in society, for the renewal and unity of mankind;

sends men into the world equipped to prepare the way for God's rule on earth by proclaiming freedom to the captives and sight to the blind;

awakens Christians to watch for the Lord's coming, when he will judge the living and the dead, and open the gates of his city to all his people.[14]

These gifts of the Holy Spirit are received in faith and obedience; they make the churches who so believe and obey truly catholic. May this catholic spirit be reborn in Methodism—in its worship by providing a home for all sorts and conditions of men and women; in its witness by seeking for the realization of genuine humanity in rural and urban settings, among affluent peoples and among those in developing nations; and in all of its life by recognizing that organized Methodism is but a provisional instrument for the wholeness of the church and the unity of mankind.

[14] *Uppsala Report*, pp. 13-14.

viii
the road ahead for united methodists

As one member of The United Methodist Church in America, I wish to affirm that I believe the denomination has the will and resources—both financial and human—to be a creative part of the mainstream of ecumenism in our day. To be sure, formidable obstacles stand in the way of Methodism's progress along the ecumenical road. A large membership and a highly structured bureaucracy provide built-in hazards. We are constantly tempted by the illusion that we are strong enough to "go it alone." There is a tendency to become preoccupied with the oiling and operating of institutional machinery, giving only a perfunctory nod to the rapidly changing world in which we live. Nevertheless, within this large machinery and membership is a latent power which *can* be directed, trained, and then released into those currents of action, prayer, and thought which together constitute the ecumenical movement.

Surely such a development is encouraged by a long look at the mammoth complexities of the tasks to which we have traditionally directed our denominational attention and resources; even the most conservative among us will be convinced that Methodist resources can be better utilized, that better results will be more readily attained, if we seek to perform these tasks in concert with other members of the family of Christ. Such cooperation also is encouraged by Methodists' experience of fellowship embracing a variety of racial and cultural minorities in the United States and an even larger experience of work across some fifty national lines with an even larger variety of racial, language, and cultural groups.

That experience within the worldwide family of Methodists has provided a conditioning for encounter across denominational boundaries.

As a laywoman I am particularly heartened by the growing number of persons whose experience has taught them the inclusive dimensions of Christian understanding and witness required of a faithful church in today's world. That lesson has come through a variety of unheralded activities in local communities across the country. One of the most striking of these activities has been the "Living Room Dialogues" in which Protestant and Catholic laymen, meeting for conversation in each others' homes, have begun to see more clearly the possibilities of Christian unity, to understand the practical and theological differences that separate us, and at times to attempt new patterns of Christian witness in their communities.

A great assortment of ecumenical experiences is helping create what has been called the "lay doctrine of equivalence." This "doctrine" calls attention to the fact that the laity, who migrate a great deal from one denomination to another, are more concerned with the functional or practical side of church life than they are with the presumed or actual theological uniqueness of a particular denomination. They favor functional effectiveness and grow impatient with competition on "nonessentials." Their instinctive ecumenism is well expressed by the famous seventeenth-century aphorism, "In essentials, unity; in non-essentials, liberty; in all things, charity."

If The United Methodist Church is to move creatively toward its ecumenical future, several critical issues must be faced.

177

1. Seeking to Understand Faith

At this point in history, the ways a Christian can express his commitment to truth will be radically different from the ways of another generation. It is a time for listening and for dialogue and, above all, for the abandonment of pride and obsessive concern with fine points of Christian doctrine. God's avant-garde may well be those laymen whose theological understanding has led them to dispense with trivial aspects of theological debate and to focus—in an active way—on the struggle for a higher level of human existence, for the God who is hidden but alive in the revolutionary ferment of our time. These persons have little interest in talk about the death of God. They are busy seeking practical expressions of their vocation to serve him.

The direction that such service must take is increasingly evident. Where our neighbor's well-being or our own humanity is at stake, the guidelines seem clear in the New Testament teaching regarding the great commandment (Matthew 22:39; Mark 12:31; Luke 10:37) to love neighbor as self. It is hard for the convinced layman to let problems of doctrine and polity prevent him from joining forces with any others who share this conviction. What Christians could justify turning aside from fellow Christians engaged in deeds of compassion for other human beings in need and pain? Such patterns of Christian cooperation may not be sufficiently cognizant of the deeper meanings of Christian unity, but they are valid approaches; and for some, they are necessary steps toward a full understanding of the nature of the church.

No Christian of our generation has better exemplified this concern for complete involvement on the neighbor's behalf

than the late Robert Spike. When speaking of the 1963
March on Washington, he said that at no other time in his
ministry did he feel so sure that he was where he ought to
be—in the street in the midst of God's people. Bob Spike
believed, as Howard Moody said in a moving tribute at the
time of Bob's death, that the "secular celebrations of the
world may be God's epiphanies of the twentieth century."

This present-day emphasis on action has been caught well
in a poem published regularly in *Nexus*, the alumni magazine
of Boston University School of Theology.

Duties of the Clergy

by

Clarence Day

In Eastern lands the holiest gents
Are those who live at least expense.
They barely speak, they seek release
From active life in prayer and peace.

But in the Western Hemisphere
A saint must catch the public ear,
And dust about and shout and bustle,
Combining holiness and hustle.[1]

There is so much today about which committed laymen
must "shout and bustle," and it is tragic that more of them
do not join the shouting and bustling. But it also is unfor-
tunate that the teaching ministry of the churches has too frequently prepared members for denominational participation
rather than for real understanding of the Christian faith.
Among the consequences of this fact, at times, is a busy involvement in the world but without the Christian foundations
and objectives of that involvement being evident. Christians

[1] Reprinted by permission; Copr. © 1935 The New Yorker Magazine, Inc.

now involved in the world's struggles must be called to greater depths of understanding of their faith. Is it too much to hope that a mutually advantageous coalition can be established between those theologians and laymen who are committed to improving the lot of the oppressed, the despised, and the disadvantaged?

2. Church Bureaucracy and Christian Unity

Church bureaucratic structures can either assist or resist church mergers and other forms of church unity. The United Methodist Church (which only the uninformed few would contend is not a bureaucracy) has a telling history in the use of its resources in the cause of interchurch cooperation and in efforts toward church union. But it must be admitted that there have been flaws in its ecumenical participation. Some members still are suspicious, and others (a small minority) are openly scornful, of ecumenical involvement. We have not always carried our weight in interchurch ventures.

Increased commitment to Methodism's ecumenical future will come as more persons responsible for the denomination's direction reflect upon the deepest meaning of the church and its relation to contemporary history. Such reflection, I believe, indicates that there is a rhythm to time, and that the church is part of a movement that is both evolutionary and natural. This rhythm of time is creation's tempo; it is God's "good time." Creation moves, even though imperceptibly at times and not always without setbacks, in the direction of increasing community, toward unity. If any movement has characterized the twentieth century, both among secular organizations and among the churches, it has been a uniting, merging movement —witness the birth of the United Nations, the development of regional consciousness among many geo-political units, and the merger of smaller into larger business corporations. The development of the World Council of Churches, national councils, and church unions is also in this stream. To seek to reverse it and return to narrow denominationalism would be to act against history in our time.

Most bureaucrats in the administration of The United Methodist Church have thrown their status and support behind efforts to work ecumenically. This fact is so pronounced that the voice speaking against such involvement is indeed "crying in the wilderness." Most of these same bureaucrats have exerted energies on behalf of the recent union between Evangelical United Brethren and Methodists. To be sure, this union cannot be counted as a union to "heal our brokenness," for our two denominations shared such a common history in polity and organization as to make almost impossible any such claim.

But if in intradenominational unions the full interpretative resources of the bureaucratic structures are required to effect change and acceptance, how much more will they be needed to move the denomination into more far-reaching unions and quests for Christian unity? An immediate field of testing is open to us in the negotiations now under way in the Consultation on Church Union.

We must recognize that when churches, all of which have bureaucratic ailments, are to be integrated, the primary question is likely to be not what the mind of Christ requires for administrative structure but how to allocate effectively available personnel, building, and financial resources in order to expedite certain tasks to which the several churches already are committed. What COCU requires of United Methodists is that we resist the temptation to "settle down" with new programs resulting from the recent Methodist-EUB union. In spite of programming on "rapid social change" in society, neither national staff nor members of denominational boards are really conditioned to its occurrence in the church. They therefore may be inclined to resist any creative steps in COCU that eventually could lead United Methodists toward yet further new forms of church life. Bureaucrats—like most other human beings—rarely prefer the new over the familiar.

This bureaucratic resistance must be met effectively. Perhaps the Commission created by the 1968 Uniting General Conference to study board and agency structure can generate enough tension and excitement in the denomination to convert staff and boards from the tendencies to build empires, to encourage institutional introversion, and to do together only those things which they are unable to do separately. The study itself, or the tension and excitement it creates, may help bureaucratic administrators become servants among other servants with diverse tasks and gifts. The study also may help the boards and agencies to acquire the capacity to sense new needs and to be flexible in applying skills and resources to serve changing conditions. Growth in these dimensions by our denominational bureaucracy would be a great contribution to the negotiators in church union. For these problems *within* the denomination are, to a large degree, the same ones that operate *among* the denominations to hinder the manifestation of their unity in Christ.

3. Attractions of Secular Ecumenism

A growing number of persons believe that the ecumenical movement is not airborne until Catholics and Protestants collaborate in doing the work of the church in such worldly issues as civil and human rights, international peace, and development in the Third World. They take a dim view of dialogue on theological topics they consider to be of past interest. They ask that the churches—whether Catholic, Protestant, or Orthodox—give up focusing attention on a far-off God in the skies, and that they show their deepest concern for Christ suffering in the agonies and hurts of his people in the world.

Certainly not all Christians share this enthusiasm for secular ecumenism. Some cast a cold eye on ecumenists who speak of finding Christ in the emerging revolutions of our time; it all sounds to them so dangerously secular, as if the Christian religion had surrendered to the world.

Surely we must recognize that the secular ecumenists are in touch with the great movement for liberation and humanization now under way around the world. The civil rights movement, the peace movement, the rebellion in Communist countries are all aspects of it. That Christians have been deeply touched by it is indicated by the emergence of renewal groups, *ad hoc* communities, and innovative forms of witness and mission. The distinctive marks of this "underground church" have been helpfully described by Fr. George Hafner, a member of an experimental parish in Trenton, New Jersey. They include a search for a new style of Christian life and for a new form of Christian presence in the world; the crossing of denominational lines as Christians to work together, to stand with man in his struggle for the humanization of society; preference for *ad hoc* committees and provisional structures rather than new institutional structures; distinguishing between lay and clergy only as a distinction of function within the church community, with both viewed as having equal responsibility for the world; and recognition of Christianity as a revolutionary movement.[2]

Secularity, as a way of understanding Christian existence today, is shaking the foundations of sacred ecclesiastical institutions, and the secular ecumenists are questioning the adequacy of traditional ecumenical assumptions and organizations. They want to be with Christ wherever he is renewing the world. Consequently they believe that Christians should gather here and there, not necessarily in temples, but often in tents or newly developed shanty towns, in pilgrim communities which form temporarily wherever they find occasion to communicate and to celebrate a breakthrough in man's existence. These secular ecumenists overrun the false boundaries between church and nonchurch institutions, thereby helping us to see more clearly what and where the church really is.

Rosemary Ruether, a Roman Catholic laywoman, has succinctly stated the mission of those Christians who today constitute the "underground church."

If the gospel is really to be a good news for the whole man, then it has to break out of that corner created by the secularization of society and the retreat of the church into the private umbilical sector of man's life. It must move into the fullness of man's existence, but it cannot do this as a churchly institution, but only in some new and entirely different form which abrogates the distinction between sacred and secular institutions, a distinction that has been created by the self-mythologies of church and non-church institution alike. It must decisively alter the very

[2] "A New Style of Christianity," *Commonweal*, May 31, 1968, pp. 331-34.

meanings of communion and ministry, church and mission, to break these realities out of the corner where they are but are not, and reveal them where they are thought not to be and yet are. It is precisely to this task that the free church, the church which is conscious of being the Christian community and yet decisively breaks out of the mold of historic church organizations, is now called.[3]

Secular ecumenists usually have not hesitated to enter into coalitions with persons of other religions. In most of the developing nations, where Christianity is a minority religion, Christians have struggled for nationhood side by side with Muslims, Hindus, and Buddhists. In our own land Protestants and Catholics have joined with Jews in the struggle for human rights. By doing so they have reopened the Jewish-Christian dialogue. No encounter, unless it be that between Christians and Muslims, raises as many questions for the churches as the Jewish-Christian encounter.

Fr. Gregory Baum has analyzed this matter closely and concludes that the challenge of the Jewish-Christian dialogue falls into two major categories—the church's understanding of its own mission and its understanding of Jewish religion. Does dialogue with Jews compromise the Christian mission? Is Jewish religion Old Testament religion and hence only prelude to New Testament faith? Or does Judaism remain a living part of God's plan of salvation for man? [4]

Will those Christian laymen caught up in secular ecumenism find ways to contribute to the renewal of this dialogue?

[3] "Schism of Consciousness," *Commonweal*, May 31, 1968, p. 329.
[4] "The Doctrinal Basis for Jewish-Christian Dialogue," *The Ecumenist*, May-June, 1968, pp. 145-52.

Perhaps they can do so best by saying, as Wesley did, "if thy heart is as my heart, give me thy hand."

Secular ecumenism holds promise for the churches' renewal, but one must also admit that it may provide capable laymen a too easily accessible avenue of witness outside the institutional structures of the church—to the comfort of those who would keep the church comfortable! It is my strong hope that the channels and resources of the church will be sufficiently open to allow them to be used freely by groups eager to move out into the world in Christ's name. The ecclesiastical ecumenists and the secular ecumenists dare not go completely separate ways.

4. Models of Ecumenical Development

In spite of criticism we may hear about the ecumenical movement, it is enjoying a great expansion of interest. In fact, some wonder if, in the face of radical new attempts at church renewal, the traditional ecumenical institutions can keep pace with the fervor for ecumenism. Criticisms aimed at denominational bureaucracies are also directed toward the "ecumenical establishment." Since the aim of the ecumenical movement is not bigger and better schools, hospitals, and churches but a new vision of the mission of the church to the world, I believe it can avoid the usual difficulties of an establishment.

The diverse models guiding current ecumenical development indicate a healthy atmosphere of experimentation and unwillingness to settle for any one form. Some of these models should be noted.

Among theological seminaries, one now sees a growing

effort to pool facilities, faculties, and curricula for the sake of educating students in a setting that is richer both ecumenically and intellectually. Such arrangements can allow agreements and disagreements to be better understood, give students a profitable interchange in field work experiences, and facilitate graduates' adaptation to possible new forms of ecumenical ministry.

Churches involved in the missionary pilgrimage have been forced by social and political developments in both nation and world to reassess their service, their methods of performance, and their involvement with the people served. This is true whether in an inner-city setting in the United States or a similar one in Uganda. It is to the credit of the missionary enterprise and to the advantage of the ecumenical movement that the difficulties experienced by early missionary effort and the evolutionary (now revolutionary) development of nations and people forced the churches to unity, or at least to work in the spirit of unity, in order to remain engaged in mission.

United colleges, hospitals, churches, and orphanages resulted in many parts of the nation and world. They stand today as reminders that the mission of service to people in need must overrule denominational differences.

Calls for autonomy by overseas churches and demands for inclusion by racial and cultural minorities at home have required denominations to search for new models of action and response. Will we United Methodists hold fast to our "religious colonies" in the interest of a deeper worldwide denominationalism? For those who answer "yes" the question is "how?" Will we free ourselves from red tape and retarded mission approaches in order to bring racial, cultural, and language minorities in the United States into the mainstream of decision-making about what the church's policies should be? For those who answer "yes" the question is "how?"

The urgency of the latter problem is underlined by the rapid rise of "black caucus" groups in predominantly white religious bodies. In less than a year, nine such groups have developed across the country: Black Methodists for Church Renewal (United Methodist Church), the Black Affairs Council (Unitarian-Universalist Association), the Union of Black Clergy and Laity (Protestant Episcopal Church), the American Baptist Convention Black Caucus (American Baptist Convention), the Black Lutheran Caucus (American Lutheran Church, United Lutheran Church, and Lutheran Church—Missouri Synod), Concerned Presbyterians (United Presbyterian Church), the Black Caucus of the Presbyterian Church in the U.S., Black Clergy United (United Church of Christ), and the Black Caucus of the Roman Catholic Church.[5]

The Delta Ministry, a project sponsored by the National Council of Churches in Mississippi, has been a tension-creating model in many parts of the church, more because of certain sectional, psychological "in feelings" than the approach it makes to people in need. This arena of action has won the support of those in the denominations who share a commitment to the struggle for justice. Some denominations chose to be part of this ministry, but others did not.

5. Possibilities for Methodists

The future offers United Methodists both opportunities and risks. We must not become so engrossed in movements

---

[5] *National Council of Negro Churchmen Newsletter*, June, 1968.

toward union and autonomy with our overseas counterparts that we lessen our zeal for negotiations with the United States–based Consultation on Church Union. Likewise, our concern for the structure of United Methodism overseas must not be allowed to overshadow our need for serious conversations about union with the three black Methodist denominations in this country. And we must keep in proper perspective our relationship with a world Methodist organization and our responsiblity in the World Council of Churches

Although no one can say with any certainty where the road ahead will lead United Methodists, we can distinguish several very big obstacles in that road. One major stumbling block for a denomination as large and wealthy as ours is its sheer self-sufficiency. This is perhaps a greater obstacle than denominational pride, devotion to a particular polity, or mistaken ideas of doctrinal purity. We are simply so big, efficient, wealthy, and devoted to pragmatic results that we do not encounter those compelling nontheological factors which drive some smaller churches to seek union. When we see some large task that needs our attention, we mobilize our vast machinery and go to work under some quadrennial tag like "A New Church for a New World" and set about confidently to raise our twenty million dollars and recruit our volunteers. But do we really discuss in advance with other Christians or secularists with similar goals how the money should be spent and the volunteers used? Do we not characteristically whip our organization into shape and then announce the results and perhaps even offer the resources to others?

Another danger that confronts United Methodists is our ambivalence about world confessionalism. Some even fear The United Methodist Church is seeking a kind of ecclesiastical *Pax Americana*. Tracey Jones has denied that this is our intent; but he also has recognized that "it is certainly true that the British Methodists see in many of our recent pronouncements about the world Methodist church the danger of a new style of world confessionalism that is supported by American money and drive."[6] The best way to protect ourselves from these charges and from the latent temptation, Dr. Jones says, is to be sure that all our planning and thinking is done in an ecumenical setting. The real question is whether even such a loose temporary structure bringing Methodists from Europe, North America, Asia, Australia, Africa, and Latin America into a new confederation is an anachronism.

Another important question arising from our world missionary patterns is whether The United Methodist Church is willing to surrender its decision-making powers over former mission churches and continue to give them support. Are the new programs we are projecting in areas such as development and urbanization only a more sophisticated form of imperialism replacing our old mother-daughter relationships? Are churches overseas in turn willing to give up their privileges and monetary advantages for freedom and autonomy from mission boards, and would they put whatever energy was thereby released into local and regional ecumenical channels?

Is the Board of Missions willing, and is the famous "man in the pew" ready, to give up institutional identity in order to pool resources and personnel for "Joint Action for Mission" as defined by the World Council of Churches' Division of World Mission and Evangelism in 1963? Under this plan all the churches and mission boards in an area would, for ex-

[6] Presentation by Dr. Tracey K. Jones, Jr., at Northeastern Jurisdictional Conference, July 25, 1968.

ample, survey needs and existing facilities and then decide perhaps to close all but one hospital in the area and support that one jointly. So far, little enthusiasm has been shown for this ecumenical ideal by any denomination.

Long before comprehensive organizational and doctrinal unity is accomplished, many things could be done together by the churches which are now done separately. The time has come for Methodists to pioneer by giving up some of our own ways. It has long been the habit of denominations to withhold all but small amounts of money from ecumenical organizations working in areas such as mission and communications, and then to give those organizations' inability to produce as the reason for the continuation of separate denominational programming. How many institutions, magazines, curriculum plans, and program materials would we be willing to unite with others—bearing all the headaches of cooperation? It is tragic to look at all the denominational items which are produced to perpetuate a denomination's brand name and peculiar twists and kinks—but which in fact are either identical in content with other such items or separately mediocre. We could liberate an enormous amount of time, energy, and money if denominations were ever able to surrender their separate identities and trust some highly competent individuals to work for them all. Because interdenominational cooperation in the past has often meant lowest common denominator compromise, we all fear joint mediocrity. But let's face it: we have costly dullness and mediocrity now in many separate endeavors.

All across the world, including the United States, there is more demand for decision-making and program development to occur on the local level. This hurts us connectionalminded Methodists, but if we are wise we will see the possibility for a new kind of connectionalism less involved with passing down program from headquarters than with helping local units, who have taken risks, establish links of community laterally—from city to rural area, from nation to nation.

The Uppsala Assembly of the World Council of Churches helped us see how the unity and catholicity of congregations and denominations easily become confused with (and compromised by) other solidarities and communities. This confusion occurs wherever Christian communities

allow the Gospel to be obscured by prejudices which prevent them from seeking unity;

allow their membership to be determined by discrimination based on race, wealth, social class or education;

do not exhibit in all the variety of their life together the essential oneness in Christ of men and women;

allow cultural, ethnic, or political allegiances to prevent the organic union of churches which confess the same faith within the same region;

prescribe their own customary practices as binding on other Christians as the condition for cooperation and unity;

permit loyalty to their own nation to hinder or to destroy their desire for mutual fellowship with Christians of another nation.[7]

United Methodists could do worse than to judge themselves by these criteria!

[7] *Uppsala Report*, pp. 14-15.

ix
summoned to mission

The destiny of Methodism in an ecumenical age is to summon the whole church to mission. The world mission of Jesus, far from being finished, has scarcely begun. Methodism, whether in ecumenical cooperation or by losing itself in organic church union, must offer with all Christians a response of obedience to the commission of Jesus to proclaim the gospel to all mankind.

Methodism was brought into being by God to recall the church to the primacy of the mission of Jesus in the world. In the eighteenth century, as in many another hour in church history, Christians had turned their backs on mission. The church, complacent, inward looking, cared not that men lived and died without a knowledge of Jesus Christ. Through Methodism, in England and across the seas, God sent forth new messengers to be carriers of the gospel. By his creative act in begetting Methodism, God renewed the whole church in mission.

After all, Methodism has no unique contribution to offer the whole church in doctrine or in church polity. From the beginning and throughout its history, it has moved within the mainstream of Christian thought and theology. Methodism is a mood, an accent, a stance, a spirit, a dynamic driving movement. It reveals its authentic self in mission, primarily and always in mission.

The whole world today cries out for mission. Millions of people in the older areas which once were called Christendom live perpetually beyond the influence of the institutional church and know nothing of the good news of Jesus.

Alienated from traditional forms of Christianity, the gospel for them remains hidden.

Beyond Christendom are two billion people who have not yet been reached by the gospel. Because of the population explosion they are being added to by the million every week. Much is rightly heard of the threat to mankind's physical welfare by the expected doubling of world population to six billion people in thirty years. All too little is heard of the significance spiritually to the people and of the consequences for the church of this vast multiplication of population. Before such facts the Christian church faces the greatest challenge of its long history.

Now mission is everywhere. It is part of the challenge of all six continents. There are no "giving" and "receiving" churches any more. People who do not know Christ belong to the concrete jungles of all cities no less than to the green jungles of Asia and Africa.

William Temple once said: "We are the early Christians." And we are. The dimensions and the complexity of the world mission of Jesus are greater than ever before. The task of making God's Son, Jesus Christ, known to all men is inescapably the supreme summons facing the Christian church today.

Methodism's evangelical, missionary passion is as urgent and as relevant as ever it was. There are disturbing signs appearing that at the very moment of its greatest need in large segments of the church, concern for mission is in eclipse. Someone, some group of Christians, must relay the tocsin call of Jesus: "Go into all the world and preach the gospel to every creature."

As I move along the world Christian frontier, I want at

many points to cry: "Danger!" Something serious is happening to the faith and mood of some sections of the church. Some Christians are so obsessed by the truth that God is at work in the world that they seem ready to disband the church and allow it to be absorbed by the world. Some are so certain that a Christian "presence" is enough that all witness to personal belief and commitment is muted. Some are so eager to cooperate with non-Christians in a pluralistic society that Christian faith evaporates in a new kind of "Christian pantheism." In it all the Christian gospel is in danger of being betrayed by an eclecticism which leaves mankind with no Christ as universal Savior and Lord.

The ecumenical movement itself needs constantly to be reminded of the primacy of mission. The search for Christian unity, necessary and urgent as it is, has almost at times become a substitute for mission. Any call for reunion faces the peril of turning the churches in upon themselves. It is easy to imagine falsely that some new internal structural rearrangement will automatically bring new life.

Bluntly it must be said that there is little objective evidence that Christian unity of itself means power or vigor in mission. In some societies where the church is virtually undivided, as in countries where Roman Catholicism or Orthodoxy dominates, or in Protestant lands such as Sweden, there is little virility in mission. In some cases where organic unity has occurred, no added observable quickening in mission can be seen.

The World Council of Churches itself in twenty years of existence has many achievements to its credit, but in missionary concern its record is less notable. It might have been expected that the Fourth Assembly at Uppsala, following the integration of the World Council with the International Missionary Council seven years before, would show a new missionary dynamic. It was not to be. The Uppsala statements on "Renewal in Mission" are among the poorest that emerged. The ecumenical movement has not yet found its soul in mission.

Ezekiel's dramatic vision of the valley of the dry bones is painfully, probingly relevant to the present condition of ecumenical Christianity. In Ezekiel's vision the scattered bones of the skeletons in the valley came together. Skin and sinew and flesh were added to them. But still they lay help-less, lifeless. The Bible comments: "There was no breath in them." Then something happened which made all the differ-ence: "The breath came into them, and they lived, and stood upon their feet, an exceeding great host" (Ezekiel 37:10).

Ecumenical unity can be little more than the coming to-gether of "dry bones." Even organic unity of itself does not place the church upon its feet, living and breathing in strength. Something more is needed. The Spirit must come.

God has led his church into the ecumenical age not for the sake of the church, but for the sake of the world. The purpose of reunion is mission. This is perfectly clear in the high priestly prayer of Jesus in the seventeenth chapter of John's Gospel. Jesus prayed that his disciples may be one, "that the world may believe." Reunion has one overmas-tering aim: to advance the mission of Jesus in the world. God, through the ecumenical movement, is regrouping his church that it may become an instrument for the next great thrust forward of the kingdom of God on earth.

The responsibility of Methodism is to hold constantly before the eyes of the whole church the vision of mission.

This responsibility can be discharged in two ways. In some parts of the world it will mean that Methodism must press on urgently toward full organic unity with other branches of the Christian church. In other areas Methodism can best sustain its witness to mission in cooperative separate existence within the church catholic.

God's will is Christian unity. Sometimes this rightful claim is followed by the assertion that only in full organic union can God's purpose in the world be fulfilled. The ecumenical movement is certainly God's doing. Yet his ways are inscrutable and unpredictable. It is salutary to remember that at the very time when his Spirit has been drawing together the severed Body of Christ, he also has been bringing into being a new church, namely the world Pentecostal movement, with a present constituency of twenty million persons gathered since 1900.

If Methodism's destiny in an ecumenical age can be fulfilled in two ways, what guidelines can be discerned to point the way it must take at different times and places? The test is mission. There are situations where organic union with a heavily institutionalized and powerfully entrenched church would seem to mean absorption, the extinction of a passion for mission. In this case it is conceivable that God's will is for Methodism's witness to be given in separation. There are other situations where the continuation of Methodism would mean competition, a wasting of resources, and an inhibiting of mission. Methodism must listen intently and obey faithfully whatever the Spirit may say. There is no other way than to live in each situation by guidance of the Spirit.

How shall Methodism be faithful to its destiny of mission? What treasures, ancient and modern, can it offer to the

197

common heritage of Christians? In what ways shall Methodism strengthen the whole church in mission?

1. Reconciliation with God

Christianity exists to bring all mankind into a reconciled relationship with God. Jesus lived and died and rose again to end man's basic estrangement from God. The church has committed to it a ministry of reconciliation. Its primary privilege is to proclaim to all men: "Be reconciled to God."

Methodism was born through a rediscovery of the centrality of reconciliation with God. It began in the vivid, warm, personal encounter of God with John and Charles Wesley. Hence John Wesley's famous confession: "My heart was strangely warmed." In the power of a personal religious experience Methodist preachers moved out across England, America, and the world.

World Methodism rests on the foundation of the reality of reconciliation with God. From it comes not only the fact but the knowledge of sins forgiven. Following conversion comes growth, the appearance of "fruits of the Spirit." Methodism advanced in the power of transformed personalities.

There is need today for considerable sections of well-established churches to be recalled to the centrality and reality of personal religious experience. It is easy to forget that the vast structure of the church stands on a simple, single event: one man's, one woman's encounter with God. Religion too often is formalized. Secondary concerns in the church take precedence over primary issues. Ritual, church organization, and the nurture of the faithful crowd out evangelism. It is forgotten that conversion, the winning of people to a first experience of God in Christ, is the heart of everything.

As the ecumenical family grows, the World Council of Churches needs to receive the emphasis on experiential faith which confessional Methodism has to make. The entrance of the Eastern Orthodox into the ecumenical movement has greatly strengthened the witness of ancient rituals and liturgical practices. Moving closer to the World Council is the Roman Catholic Church, bringing with it a further heavy emphasis on tradition and the church as an institution. As a result the Protestant interpretation of the Christian faith in terms of directness, simplicity, and the primacy of personal religious experience could become submerged. Methodism, as one heir of the Reformation, has a vital contribution to make to ecumenical Christianity by defining religious faith as personal.

The call to personal commitment to Christ is especially relevant in an age of religious indifferentism and recession. At a time when children grow up in Christian homes and society accepts Christian truth, it is understandable that programs of Christian education and nurture take precedence in Christian planning. When millions must be confronted for the first time with the gospel, the call to conversion becomes paramount. The supreme task is to get men and women to commence the Christian life.

In seeking the reconciliation of man to God, Methodism must call for a new stance in commitment. In the past, Methodist preachers have called the people to the foot of the cross of Jesus, bidding them kneel and look up that perpendicular arm of the cross into the face of God. Today the eyes of all who are confronted with Christ must be focused at the point where the two crossbeams meet. There we must all be held, nailed by the love of God for us. There we

199

must also be nailed in compassion for our fellows, our world, and summoned to action for our neighbor's sake. Only as each one of us remains at the focal point where the perpendicular and horizontal beams of the cross meet shall we be obedient to the Christ whose word commands us today.

Methodism's understanding of personal reconciliation with God, of the reality of conversion, is vital to the health of a church which dares to go out in faith to the people. God may well be trusting Methodism, in a new obedience to its historic understanding of the gospel, to hold before the whole church the necessity and the fact of conversion. Right now Methodism's destiny could be to show the church and the world the power which comes from personal reconciliation with God.

2. The Call to Holiness

Historically the marks of a Methodist are personal piety, disciplined living, and social holiness. In this new age it is the task of Methodism to show the world a way of faith and a way of life.

Long before the modern phrase was coined, Methodism knew the meaning of "worldly holiness." Roman Catholic saintliness was centered in the monasteries where it was nurtured in withdrawal from life. Early Methodism sought holiness in the midst of the world. In a sense all Methodism became an extension of the "Holy Club" of Oxford University which was so much a part of the early experience of the Wesleys. Daily prayer and Bible study, a piety which drew back from the impurities and grossness of a corrupt society, and care for the dispossessed became features of the Methodist way of life. As a result streams of cleansing water were set flowing which quickened personal religion and revived a decaying morality.

Religious impotence and moral permissiveness are characteristic of today's society. In a noisy, fast-moving era personal devotional piety is difficult. Sunday as a "day of rest and worship" is largely gone. There is a crisis in worship, and prayer as talking with God is practiced by few Christians. Modern Christians in a secular society find it almost impossible to "take time to be holy."

Moral permissiveness is sweeping over Western society. We are unable to handle the new freedom which has come in man-woman relationships, or to cope with scientific developments such as "the pill." An upthrust of sexuality threatens to contaminate the very fountains of living. With indiscipline of the instincts, compulsive social diseases such as alcoholism and obsessive gambling cloud the lives of millions.

In this kind of world the witness of Methodism to personal acts of devotion and disciplined living is far from irrelevant. How shall the joy of worship, the peace of personal prayer, and the positive values of a Christian Sunday be demonstrated save by Christians who follow this way of life? How shall sexual corruption be halted if there are none whose lives act as a barrier against the tainted imagination and acts of sexual impurity? How shall people be reminded that there is a better way of living than by being slaves to the desires and appetites of the flesh except through people who show the triumph of inner freedom?

Today, personal holiness is not enough. A larger, social holiness is the need of the world. The world requires men and women who will hate racism and war as earlier Methodists rejected liquor and gambling. The man for others, the man who finds privilege unbearable, the man who seeks dignity and justice for all God's people—that man comes nearer to New Testament saintliness.

John Wesley believed God brought Methodism into being primarily to spread "scriptural holiness through the land." It is a continuing task of Methodism. It is another contribution Methodism has to make to the church and to the world.

3. The Offer of Fellowship

Religion must be functional or it is nothing. Unless the Christian faith becomes integrated with life in the world, touching people at every level of their being, it ceases to be a living part of the world. Unless the Christian church is a relevant, creative fellowship amid the people, it becomes an optional, expendable extra to life.

Why did Methodism spread so rapidly along the moving frontiers of earlier American and Australian history? It was in part because it offered to lonely, isolated people a lively fellowship. In group religious activity from class meetings to camp meetings, in the warmth of its hymn singing, in the social as well as the religious satisfactions of worship, real needs were met. Methodism, to use an Australian word, offered "mateship."

Modern Methodism has not lost its community characteristics. The often despised activist programs of neighborhood churches are not as absurd as they sometimes sound. They provide fellowship amid the barrenness of suburbia. The church which is a community center of the people, where it is real, is truly a servant church. Methodist fellowship is a recognizable characteristic in many a town or city around the world.

Large segments of the Christian church know little of functional religion. The typical picture of the church in Sweden, for example, is a place of worship surrounded by gravestones. Nothing much apart from worship can happen. Religion is religion alone. I suspect this is one reason why fewer people worship in Sweden than in most countries in the world.

Modern man is a lonely man. Mass society robs people of identity, dignity, worth. The emergence of an "apartment civilization" in the large cities of the world is a basic cause of personal and social distortions of our time. High-rise apartments, with people stacked one above the other, look and are suspiciously like vertical human filing cabinets.

Loneliness has become a deep modern sickness of soul. The cities of the world are filled with rootless, isolated people. Like grains of sand, weathered, disintegrated from the rocks of which they formed a part, millions of people live an existence separated from their fellows and their community. Lives touch, like grains of sand on a beach, but have no relationship, no fellowship one with the other.

In this kind of developing society Methodism's homely communities of people have a strange relevance. A religious life that is "folksy" rather than austere, emotionally warm rather than intellectually cold, spontaneous rather than patterned and repressed is the need of millions. Methodism, because of its belief, practice, and history, is peculiarly equipped to offer this kind of Christ-based community. It is another of the gifts it has to offer ecumenical Christianity.

203

4. The Way of Service

A church which only worships, dies. Unless the church becomes the servant church in action, it has no power among men. Worship issuing in work, communion in service, withdrawal being followed always by involvement—this is the way forward.

A sure way for a church to become impotent is for it to be satisfied with being only a talking and verbalizing institution. Around the world there are all too many churches which have been maneuvered into this kind of stance. From them the people have turned away in disappointment and disillusion.

There are today in Western cities those who claim that the welfare state has made the serving ministry of the church unnecessary. Service, it is said, is better done by governments, for only governments have the financial resources sufficient for the task.

This argument is fallacious on two counts. First, there are areas of need in modern society which the secular state has not yet discovered. It is the church, at work down among the people, inspired by the compassionate spirit of Jesus, which is likely to discern need and which possesses the dedicated people able to find answers to need.

Second, there is a dimension of service which only the church can offer. Take, for example, work among the aged. A welfare state can certainly care physically for senior people; but the greatest need of the aged is for a sense of purpose and hope. It is the Christian faith which points to the great hope of eternal life. There is a vast difference in atmosphere between a secular and a truly Christian aged persons' home.

To believe that you have one foot in the grave cannot be compared with the faith that as life draws to its close you have one foot in heaven.

An example of the significance and power of the servant church can be drawn from Sydney, Australia. There in 1963 a new ministry began among the people called Life Line. It is a round-the-clock telephone service which says to the city: "Help is as close as the telephone." The telephones are staffed by trained, dedicated men and women known as telephone counselors. Behind them is available greater professional assistance, where answers in depth may be found.

Since the Life Line Centre opened, an ocean of unsuspected need has been uncovered. Some fourteen thousand first-contact calls are received annually. They range from simple loneliness to suicidal despair. Life Line, now established in other Australian cities and spreading to other countries, is fashioning a network of compassion in cities around the world.

Australian Methodism is today emphasizing the importance of service on the congregational level. Congregations, rather than denominational committees and boards, are being encouraged to find ways of serving the communities in which they exist. In other words, the same people who worship are being challenged themselves to serve.

On the international level, through such projects as Inter-Church Aid, Christians are learning afresh the importance of service. In local areas the lesson has still to be learned and obeyed. Methodism, as in Australia, is reminding the larger church that mission is fulfilled in the world when all Christians become humble servants of the humble Christ.

5. A Prophetic Ministry

Social service without social action can be mere escapism. It can be worse. By temporarily easing the lot of suffering people it can perpetuate injustice. The servant church must be the prophetic church.

Prophetic witness has been part of Methodism since its earliest beginnings. John Wesley played a worthy part in the eighteenth-century struggle against the institution of slavery. The last letter he wrote before his death was to William Wilberforce, urging him to be unresting until slavery was banished from the earth.

Similarly, John Wesley preached and wrote against war. Some of his statements in their biting irony and passion are precursors of modern-day Christian peacemakers.

Modern Methodism, often traditional and institution-alized, is not without its strong prophetic voices. In England, America, and Australia, individual Methodists and, less frequently, church pronouncements and actions have taken their place at the growing edge of the conscience of society.

Methodism is at once personal and social. At many moments and places in its history tension has emerged from this twofold aspect of the gospel. That tension is present today. By maintaining the tension, by seeking a synthesis between personal piety and social witness, Methodism speaks strongly to today's church and today's world. By holding both in balance, Methodism has a vital contribution to make to the whole church in an ecumenical age.

Mankind has entered a period when in world affairs the voice of prophetic religion must be heard. Without it humanity could be plunged into violent world revolution and world war.

The Uppsala Assembly of the World Council of Churches revealed the depth of the gulf which today divides mankind. Humanity is not now primarily divided between Russia and America, the East and the West. Now the world's dangerous and growing conflict is between rich and poor nations, the white and the colored, developed and developing nations. It is the conflict between the one billion who have everything and the two billion, the Third World, which has nothing. In this struggle Russia is lumped with America, and both are confronted by the people of Asia, Africa, and Latin America. Time is running out for Northern man with his white skin, his wealth, and his power. The march of the poor, led perhaps presently by China, moves challengingly into history.

Three great world issues are converging, creating a massive revolutionary ferment. They are the questions of poverty, race, and war. It seems as if suddenly millions of people have made up their minds they have had enough of this kind of world. No longer is poverty to be endured. The structures of capitalism must be changed. Racial discrimination must end, and end quickly. The revolt against war has begun. Youths by the thousands are refusing to take up arms. Never again will America or any nation be able to mount a war like Vietnam.

A time of revolution is a time of prophecy. The church must not again be found, as so often in the past, on the wrong side of revolutionary change. Methodism carries responsibility to try to disentangle the people's thought and emotion from unquestioning attachment to the status quo.

Methodism, by prophetically pointing to the future, can aid the whole church to move with the Spirit of God as he fashions a new humanity.

Each of these five features outlined appears in authentic Methodism. Through the power of the Holy Spirit they are bound together in a seamless whole. It is the privilege of Methodism, by being true to itself, to offer these gifts to the common storehouse of the total church of Jesus Christ.

In the renewal of the church, God always uses the gifts available from the past and the present. There is always a continuity between yesterday and tomorrow. The new is compounded in part of the old. Yet it is new. No one can foresee as yet the pattern of the new church which will be adequate to the new world now emerging.

God in our time will renew his church. He is renewing it now. In many places around the world the deadness of the church seems to be infecting and contaminating the gospel. The hour is coming when the health of the gospel will break through, carrying vitality and life again to the church.

The Spirit of God has not forgotten or abandoned his world. Christ has not rejected his church as the instrument for advancing the kingdom of God on earth. It is the task, the destiny of Methodism in this age, in unity with the whole church, to respond in obedience to the challenge of the world mission of Jesus.